A BOOK OF
REVELATIONS

A BOOK OF
REVELATIONS

His Light Unto My Path
Ephesians 3: 1-7

A tool for study, Bible needed

VALERIA FRANKLIN

ARPress

ARPress
45 Dan Road Suite 5
Canton MA 02021

Hotline: 1(888) 821-0229
Fax: 1(508) 545-7580

Ordering Information:
Quantity sales. Special discounts are available on quantity purchases by corporations, associations, and others. For details, contact the publisher at the address above.

Printed in the United States of America.

ISBN-13:   Paperback   979-8-89389-090-7
               eBook   979-8-89389-091-4
               Hardcover   979-8-89389-092-1

Library of Congress Control Number: 2024909343

Table of Contents

Salutation

For this cause I Valeria, the prisoner of Jesus Christ for you who believe, If you will hear of the dispensation of the grace of God which is given me to you-ward:

How that by revelation He made known unto me the mystery; (as I wrote afore in God's Plan For Me, becoming sons and daughters of God, Whereby, when ye read, ye may understand my knowledge in the mystery of Christ

Which in other ages was not made known unto the sons of men, as it is now revealed unto His holy apostles and prophets by the Spirit;

That the you should be fellowheirs, and of the same body, and partakers of his promise in Christ by the gospel:

Whereof I was made a minister, according to the gift of the grace of God given unto me by the effectual working of His power.

Foundation of Ephesians 3:1-7

Introduction

Revelation is given for where we are going not where we are; to build our confidence in our God. With confidence we can stand, resting assured, that what God promised is what it shall be no matter what the present state. Calling those things that be not, as though they were. Declaring the ending from the beginning.

The problem is that God can not reveal to us the latter end if we are not going anywhere. We have to be in active pursuit of Him, not happiness. Seeking first His Kingdom and His righteousness, then all these things (the things that make us happy) shall be added unto us. Yet, even in revealing His divine will, it takes **obedience**, which Jesus learned by the things He suffered. The one thing most of us are not willing to do! Because revelation comes with a price, most of us will never tap into the depth of what God has for us. This depth comes only with a close relationship (walk) with God. This cost requires paying up front from the beginning and continuing to pay up front. There is no credit and promise to pay, nor is there a lay-a-way plan. We must pay up front in full, forsaking all, denying ourselves, taking up our crosses daily and following Him. Hearkening diligently. He has promised that no man that has left houses, or brethern, or sisters, or father, or mother, or wife, or children, or lands, for my sake and the gospel's sake, But he shall receive an hundredfold now in this lifetime houses and brethern and sisters and mothers and children, and lands, with persecutions; and in the world to come eternal life.

Persecutions, another word most of us want no parts of. The very sufferings that we partake of are centered around persecution. So while some never get started, many others don't finish. Many are called but few are chosen. When we get the revelation of chosen, then we learn that quitting is not an option. The book was written before the movie was made. It's already in the script, all we have to do is walk it out. **Walk It Out, Walk It Out!**

I

Chosen

For I know the thoughts I think towards you, saith the Lord, thoughts of peace and not of evil, to give you an expected end. **Jeremiah 29:11**

The Call

Many have confused the call as to be the assignment or purpose. The call is to come closer, to a place of undivided attention, a place where the Father can speak with us. Just as when God called Abram; "Get thee out of thy country and from they kindred, and from thy father's house, unto a land that I will shew thee". This was not a physical place to start. It was a spiritual place to later be manifested in the natural. This place must first be seen in the spirit, a place of undivided attention, where assignments are given, leading to purpose, His expected end.

The call meaning come here, come close to me, I want to show you something.

On August of 1997, the call came to me, to come closer for instructions, just as Abram. To leave a place of comfort in pursuit of a place promised, not yet seen. After receiving instructions with clarity, on January 1998, I made that step that changed my life forever. To enter a way of life that would stretch my faith continuously, never going back to the way life was.

Isaiah 49:10 - 51:16, The voice of His servant Isaiah, "he that walketh in darkness and hath no light". A walk of faith; darkness here not being the darkness of this world, but as to what many might call blind faith. A call to walk according to the word, by faith and not by sight. Just as Abram was called out, by the voice, words of God, not knowing where he was going, but yet "trusting in the name of the Lord and staying (not leaving) upon his God. On target!

Vs11

Behold, all ye that kindle a fire, that compass yourselves about with sparks: walk in the light of your fire, and in the sparks that ye have kindled. This shall ye have of mine hand; ye shall lie down in sorrow.

You, that trust in your own works; what you can do and have accomplished. Job, education, material gain, etc. What has been birthed out of your will and way. To hold on to your will and way, will only bring sorrow by the hand of God. Once the call comes, this becomes contrary to the will of God and will work against you. Just as when Jesus chose his Disciples, they had to walk away from great professions. One was a physician, a lawyer, a tax collector, they all were entrepreneurs, but the call required them to give it all up and follow him. Counting the cost of their relationship with him of greater value.

"For what profit a man to gain the whole world and lose his soul. Whosoever will save his life, shall lose it, and whosoever will lose his life for my sake shall find it."**Matt.16: 25-26. Our will must become His will!**

Isaiah 51:1-2

51:1 Hearken to me, ye that follow after righteousness, ye that seek the LORD: look unto the rock whence ye are hewn, and to the hole of the pit whence ye are digged.

2 Look unto Abraham your father, and unto Sarah that bare you: for I called him alone, and blessed him, and increased him.

Hear me, you who really trust me. Consider Abraham (the father of faith) and Sarah whose loins we came out of (seed of Abraham). For I called him **alone** (just one man's obedience, trusting God) How God blessed and increased him. All God needs is our obedience. It matters not who is with you or for you; **Rom. 8:30-31** "Moreover whom He foreknew He did predestinate, whom he did predestinate them he also called, and whom He called He also justified, and whom he justified, them He also glorified. What shall we say then to these things? If God be for us, who can be against us"?

For the LORD shall comfort Zion: he will comfort all her waste places; and he will make her wilderness like Eden, and her desert like the garden of the LORD; joy and gladness shall be found therein, thanksgiving, and the voice of melody. Isa 51:4-16

4 Hearken unto me, my people; and give ear unto me, O my nation: for a law shall proceed from me, and I will make my judgment to rest for a light of the people.

5 My righteousness is near; my salvation is gone forth, and mine arms shall judge the people; the isles shall wait upon me, and on mine arm shall they trust.

6 Lift up your eyes to the heavens, and look upon the earth beneath: for the heavens shall vanish away like smoke, and the earth shall wax old like a garment, and they that dwell therein shall die in like manner: but my salvation shall be for ever, and my righteousness shall not be abolished.

7 Hearken unto me, ye that know righteousness, the people in whose heart is my law; fear ye not the reproach of men, neither be ye afraid of their revilings.

8 For the moth shall eat them up like a garment, and the worm shall eat them like wool: but my righteousness shall be for ever, and my salvation from generation to generation.

9 Awake, awake, put on strength, O arm of the LORD; awake, as in the ancient days, in the generations of old. Art thou not it that hath cut Rahab, and wounded the dragon?

10 Art thou not it which hath dried the sea, the waters of the great deep; that hath made the depths of the sea a way for the ransomed to pass over?

11 Therefore the redeemed of the LORD shall return, and come with singing unto Zion; and everlasting joy shall be upon their head: they shall obtain gladness and joy; and sorrow and mourning shall flee away.

12 I, even I, am he that comforteth you: who art thou, that thou shouldest be afraid of a man that shall die, and of the son of man which shall be made as grass;

13 And forgettest the LORD thy maker, that hath stretched forth the heavens, and laid the foundations of the earth; and hast feared continually every day because of the fury of the oppressor, as if he were ready to destroy? and where is the fury of the oppressor?

14 The captive exile hasteneth that he may be loosed, and that he should not die in the pit, nor that his bread should fail.

15 But I am the LORD thy God, that divided the sea, whose waves roared: The LORD of hosts is his name.

16 And I have put my words in thy mouth, and I have covered thee in the shadow of mine hand, that I may plant the heavens, and lay the foundations of the earth, and say unto Zion, Thou art my people

God will comfort all your waste places. The places of sacrifice; God will provide and protect in His own way. By causing His law (word) to rest (resolve every situation) becoming a light for His people. The word, being a lamp unto our feet and a light unto our path **Ps. 118:105.** Being in right standing with God will create all we need. Obedience brings provision.

Look to God because all else will vanish away like smoke. Glory of man is as the grass that withereth and the flower fadeth because the spirit of the Lord bloweth upon it. But the word of our God standeth forever.

Isaiah 40:7-8.

Hear me, you that know me and trust me fear not the reproach of men. Neither be ye afraid of their revilings. Many a times, as in my case, the fear of man will tend to hinder us from trusting God. What man might think, say or do. But God said **"do not be afraid of man nor man's threat!"** For many will wear themselves out trying to stop you. Just as Israel, **"the more they afflicted them, the greater they grew"** Ex. 1:12. It's only a set up for God to show forth the exceeding greatness of His power to usward, according to the working of His mighty power **Eph. 1:19.**

So stand to attention and put on strength. Focus on the power of God. The same God that dried the Red Sea. Remember past victories, for God is the same yesterday, today and forever. Therefore, right in the place of our remembering and reflecting on the past victories and power of God is where we shall find strength, joy and gladness will cause all mourning to flee away.

"For the joy of the Lord is our strength" Neh. 8:10

I am He that comforteth you (protect and provide). No need to worry about what man shall do. **"The Lord is on my side, I will not fear, what can man do unto me"? Ps. 118:6**

Don't allow fear to cause you to forget the power of God. For that fear will only torment you. Satan knows that if you obey God, there is nothing that he can do with you. You are then walking in **Dominion!** "Be sober, be vigilant; because your adversary the devil, as a roaring lion, walketh about, seeking whom he may devour" **I Peter 5:8.** The enemy roars to cause you to panic and run from your place of refuge, (safety) right into his trap that he might devour you. If you move, he will get you. We must be stedfast, unmovable, always abounding in the work of the Lord. There is nothing to be worried about, the enemy can't touch you. Be still and don't be moved by the things you see. "For our light affliction, which is but for a moment, worketh for us a far more exceeding and eternal weight of glory; While we look not at the things which are seen, but at the things which are not seen: for the things which are seen are temporal; but the things which are not seen are eternal.

2 Cor 4:17-5:1

The enemy hopes that fear will stop you. He huffs and puffs, but can't blow your house down. If you obey, you are on a strong foundation. **Fear holds us captive when we allow it to control us. But our obedience sets us free, while taking fear captive**. (For the weapons of our warfare are not carnal, but mighty through God to the pulling down of strong holds;) Casting down imaginations, and every high thing that exalteth itself against the knowledge of God, and **bringing into captivity every thought to the obedience of Christ;** And having in a readiness to revenge all disobedience, when your obedience is fulfilled.

Prov 29:25

The fear of man bringeth a snare: but whoso putteth his trust in the LORD shall be safe.

Isa 51:16

And I have put my words in thy mouth, and I have covered thee in the shadow of mine hand, that I may plant the heavens, and lay the foundations of the earth, and say unto Zion, Thou art my people.

The word of God that is hidden in our hearts will manifest the inheritance settled and reserved in heaven.

Ps 119:89 For ever, O LORD, thy word is settled in heaven.

1 Peter 1:4 To an inheritance incorruptible, and undefiled, and that fadeth not away, reserved in heaven for you, God covers us with the shadow of his hand, when we **OBEY**

1 Peter 5:6-11

6 Humble yourselves therefore under the mighty hand of God, that he may exalt you in due time:

7 Casting all your care upon him; for he careth for you.

8 Be sober, be vigilant; because your adversary the devil, as a roaring lion, walketh about, seeking whom he may devour:

9 Whom resist stedfast in the faith, knowing that the same afflictions are accomplished in your brethren that are in the world.

10 But the God of all grace, who hath called us unto his eternal glory by Christ Jesus, after that ye have suffered a while, make you perfect, stablish, strengthen, settle you.

11 To him be glory and dominion for ever and ever. Amen.

The God Who Knows All

Isaiah 48:16-22

16 Come ye near unto me, hear ye this; I have not spoken in secret from the beginning; from the time that it was, there am I: and now the Lord GOD, and his Spirit, hath sent me.

17 Thus saith the LORD, thy Redeemer, the Holy One of Israel; I am the LORD thy God which teacheth thee to profit, which leadeth thee by the way that thou shouldest go.

18 O that thou hadst hearkened to my commandments! then had thy peace been as a river, and thy righteousness as the waves of the sea:

19 Thy seed also had been as the sand, and the offspring of thy bowels like the gravel thereof; his name should not have been cut off nor destroyed from before me.

20 Go ye forth of Babylon, flee ye from the Chaldeans, with a voice of singing declare ye, tell this, utter it even to the end of the earth; say ye, The LORD hath redeemed his servant Jacob.

21 And they thirsted not when he led them through the deserts: he caused the waters to flow out of the rock for them: he clave the rock also, and the waters gushed out.

22 There is no peace, saith the LORD, unto the wicked.

The way that you should go; according to Jeremiah 29:11 the plan that He has and the steps that he has ordered for you. **The enemy cannot hold you without your permission.** Peace can only be found when we are in God's divine will. As we obey, God is obligated to deal with whatever comes against us or whatever need arises because of our obedience.

He is obligated to provide and protect. When we obey God assumes **all** responsibility. His strength is made perfect in our weakness. Not that we are sufficient of ourselves to think anything as of ourselves; but our sufficiency is of God: Who also hath made us able ministers of the new testament not of the letter, but of the spirit for the letter killeth, but the spirit giveth life. **IICorn. 3:5-6**

He is faithful to His covenant. Do your part and leave the driving up to God!

Like a river- a constant flow, nothing can interrupt your peace when you know that God has you. Your righteousness like the waves of the sea. Good things would have flowed to you like the waves of the sea. All that God has ordered at his set, appointed time. Children natural and spiritual (jobs, dreams, vision, provision; whatever God has impregnated you with through His word. We can not birth the things of God in confusion. Peace is required to hear the voice of God directing you. If we hold on to our peace (position) then God can fight our battle.

Peace eliminates distractions. Distractions cause delays. Distractions take you away from the vision. Distractions kill the anointing. Distractions take you off course, where you don't want to go!

Leave Babylon- a place of bondage, captivity; a mind set. God commands us to come out!

Peace is freedom. Anything that takes your peace has captured you and placed you in bondage.

II Cor 10:3-6

3 For though we walk in the flesh, we do not war after the flesh:

4(For the weapons of our warfare are not carnal, but mighty through God to the pulling down of strong holds;)

5 Casting down imaginations, and every high thing that exalteth itself against the knowledge of God, and bringing into captivity every thought to the obedience of Christ;

6 And having in a readiness to revenge all disobedience, when your obedience is fulfilled.

Whatever has you bound, that you cannot have peace, God says,"**Come Out!**" Just as He called Lazarus out, it's already done!

A voice of singing, praise breaks the enemy's chains. **Isa 61:3**

To appoint unto them that mourn in Zion, to give unto them beauty for ashes, the oil of joy for mourning, the garment of praise for the spirit of heaviness; that they might be called trees of righteousness, the planting of the LORD, that he might be glorified.

2 Chron 20:1-3 Jehoshaphat

20:1 It came to pass after this also, that the children of Moab, and the children of Ammon, and with them other beside the Ammonites, came against Jehoshaphat to battle.

2 Then there came some that told Jehoshaphat, saying, There cometh a great multitude against thee from beyond the sea on this side Syria; and, behold, they be Hazazon-tamar, which is En-gedi.

3 And Jehoshaphat feared, and set himself to seek the LORD, and proclaimed a fast throughout all Judah.

Jehoshaphat feared, (in bondage) so he set himself, (positioned himself) to seek the Lord, (the God who knows all).

2 Chron 20:15-17

15 And he said, Hearken ye, all Judah, and ye inhabitants of Jerusalem, and thou king Jehoshaphat, Thus saith the LORD unto you, Be not afraid nor dismayed by reason of this great multitude; for the battle is not yours, but God's.

16 To morrow go ye down against them: behold, they come up by the cliff of Ziz; and ye shall find them at the end of the brook, before the wilderness of Jeruel.

17 Ye shall not need to fight in this battle: set yourselves, stand ye still, and see the salvation of the LORD with you, O Judah and Jerusalem: fear not, nor be dismayed; to morrow go out against them: for the LORD will be with you.

The answer was, Be not afraid! The Battle is not yours, but God's. It was a set up! Then God gave him instructions, 16) To morrow go ye down against them: behold, they come up by the cliff of Ziz; and ye shall find them at the end of the brook, before the wilderness of Jeruel. God told them all they needed to know; **When, Where and How!** We serve a God of precision, no hitting and missing when we learn to do things God's way.

Even though they did not have to fight, they had to position to receive the victory. Set yourselves, stand ye still, and see the salvation of the LORD with you, O Judah and Jerusalem: fear not nor be dismayed; to morrow go out against them: for the LORD will be with you. Set, (to get in a certain place), Be still

(focus, Wherefore gird up the loins of your mind, be sober, and hope to the end for the grace that is to be brought unto you at the revelation of Jesus Christ 1 Peter 1:13; in boldness and confidence having access by faith in him Eph. 3:12)

2 Chron 20:20

And they rose early in the morning, and went forth into the wilderness of Tekoa: and as they went forth, Jehoshaphat stood and said, Hear me, O Judah, and ye inhabitants of Jerusalem; Believe in the LORD your God, so shall ye be established; believe his prophets, so shall ye prosper.

And they rose up, Obedience is the key to your victory. Even when you don't understand, just obey. Obedience is a sign of trust. Even though I don't understand Lord I believe you enough to trust you. Joyce Meyer inspired me when she said," Do it afraid!" It's not really your faith that brings the reward but your Obedience. That's why the enemy tries to stop us with fear. He knows that if we ever get to the place, in position, there's nothing he can do because now he has to battle with God himself (word), and he wants no part of that. When we obey our peace should be restored, because it's no longer our responsibility, to make it happen, but God's. Creflo Dollar said,"the pressures not on us, the pressures on God, but he doesn't receive any pressure cause he already knows". So all we have to do is **REST!**

2 Chron 20:21-22

21 And when he had consulted with the people, he appointed singers unto the LORD, and that should praise the beauty of holiness, as they went out before the army, and to say, Praise the LORD; for his mercy endureth for ever.

22 And when they began to sing and to praise, the LORD set ambushments against the children of Ammon, Moab, and mount Seir, which were come against Judah; and they were smitten.

And when they began to praise, the LORD set ambushments, our praise sets in motion the Hand of God to war on our behalf.

Isa 42:10-16

10 Sing unto the LORD a new song, and his praise from the end of the earth, ye that go down to the sea, and all that is therein; the isles, and the inhabitants thereof.

11 Let the wilderness and the cities thereof lift up their voice, the villages that Kedar doth inhabit: let the inhabitants of the rock sing, let them shout from the top of the mountains.

12 Let them give glory unto the LORD, and declare his praise in the islands.

13 The LORD shall go forth as a mighty man, he shall stir up jealousy like a man of war: he shall cry, yea, roar; he shall prevail against his enemies.

14 I have long time holden my peace; I have been still, and refrained myself: now will I cry like a travailing woman; I will destroy and devour at once.

15 I will make waste mountains and hills, and dry up all their herbs; and I will make the rivers islands, and I will dry up the pools.

16 And I will bring the blind by a way that they knew not; I will lead them in paths that they have not known: I will make darkness light before them, and crooked things straight. These things will I do unto them, and not forsake them.

God says when we praise him he will stir himself up as a mighty man of war and prevail against our enemies. For just as a pregnant woman waits for her moment and is suddenly in travail, so has He been waiting for his set (in a set place) to devour and destroy our enemies at once (suddenly). He will go forth parting waters, lowering mountains, raising valleys, making crooked things straight and rough places plain. Bringing the blind (those walking by faith and not by sight) by a way not known, **But He Knows!** He will do and not forsake us! **When we obey, it's victory every time.**

Joshua

13 And it came to pass, when Joshua was by Jericho, that he lifted up his eyes and looked, and, behold, there stood a man over against him with his sword drawn in his hand: and Joshua went unto him, and said unto him, Art thou for us, or for our adversaries?

14 And he said, Nay; but as captain of the host of the LORD am I now come. And Joshua fell on his face to the earth, and did worship, and said unto him, What saith my lord unto his servant?

15 And the captain of the LORD's host said unto Joshua, Loose thy shoe from off thy foot; for the place whereon thou standest is holy. And Joshua did so.

6:1 Now Jericho was straitly shut up because of the children of Israel: none went out, and none came in.

2 And the LORD said unto Joshua, See, I have given into thine hand Jericho, and the king thereof, and the mighty men of valour.

3 And ye shall compass the city, all ye men of war, and go round about the city once. Thus shalt thou do six days.

4 And seven priests shall bear before the ark seven trumpets of rams' horns: and the seventh day ye shall compass the city seven times, and the priests shall blow with the trumpets.

5 And it shall come to pass, that when they make a long blast with the ram's horn, and when ye hear the sound of the trumpet, all the people shall

shout with a great shout; and the wall of the city shall fall down flat, and the people shall ascend up every man straight before him.

6 And Joshua the son of Nun called the priests, and said unto them, Take up the ark of the covenant, and let seven priests bear seven trumpets of rams' horns before the ark of the LORD.

7 And he said unto the people, Pass on, and compass the city, and let him that is armed pass on before the ark of the LORD.

8 And it came to pass, when Joshua had spoken unto the people, that the seven priests bearing the seven trumpets of rams' horns passed on before the LORD, and blew with the trumpets: and the ark of the covenant of the LORD followed them.

9 And the armed men went before the priests that blew with the trumpets, and the rereward came after the ark, the priests going on, and blowing with the trumpets.

10 And Joshua had commanded the people, saying, Ye shall not shout, nor make any noise with your voice, neither shall any word proceed out of your mouth, until the day I bid you shout; then shall ye shout.

11 So the ark of the LORD compassed the city, going about it once: and they came into the camp, and lodged in the camp.

12 And Joshua rose early in the morning, and the priests took up the ark of the LORD.

13 And seven priests bearing seven trumpets of rams' horns before the ark of the LORD went on continually, and blew with the trumpets: and the armed men went before them; but the rereward came after the ark of the LORD, the priests going on, and blowing with the trumpets.

14 And the second day they compassed the city once, and returned into the camp: so they did six days.

15 And it came to pass on the seventh day, that they rose early about the dawning of the day, and compassed the city after the same manner seven times: only on that day they compassed the city seven times.

16 And it came to pass at the seventh time, when the priests blew with the trumpets, Joshua said unto the people, Shout; for the LORD hath given you the city.

17 And the city shall be accursed, even it, and all that are therein, to the LORD: only Rahab the harlot shall live, she and all that are with her in the house, because she hid the messengers that we sent.

18 And ye, in any wise keep yourselves from the accursed thing, lest ye make yourselves accursed, when ye take of the accursed thing, and make the camp of Israel a curse, and trouble it.

19 But all the silver, and gold, and vessels of brass and iron, are consecrated unto the LORD: they shall come into the treasury of the LORD.

20 So the people shouted when the priests blew with the trumpets: and it came to pass, when the people heard the sound of the trumpet, and the people shouted with a great shout, that the wall fell down flat, so that the people went up into the city, every man straight before him, and they took the city.

Now Joshua was **chosen** by God to lead the children of Isreal into the promise land. Joshua walked closely with Moses, now walking closely with God. When we are chosen to be a leader it requires that we have an intimate relationship with God, who has ordered our every step. As we walk with God, he directs us along the journey. When walking closely with God, he draws us into his presence to receive instructions, revealing to us the ending from the beginning, (who, what, where, when and sometimes why). He has ordained angels to assist us along the way.

Heb.1:14 Are not all angels ministering spirits sent to serve those who will inherit salvation?

God lets Joshua (us) know that He has "already given" the victory. It's a set up! We can trust what God says, His word! **Heb 4:3** For we which have believed do enter into rest, as he said, As I have sworn in my wrath, if they shall enter into my rest: **although the works were finished from the foundation of the world.** We have all we need in the word of God. When God gives instructions, they are precise; as in verses 3-5.

We must follow these instructions with obedience. In verse 6, Joshua called the body together to become unified. In verse 12, Joshua rose early to obey the instructions, and as the people began to shout and praise God, just as he instructed (in verse 20), the wall of Jericho fell flat. **When we obey the God who knows all, there is victory every time! No hit and misses!**

Paul and Silas

Acts 16:22

22 And the multitude rose up together against them: and the magistrates rent off their clothes, and commanded to beat them.

23 And when they had laid many stripes upon them, they cast them into prison, charging the jailer to keep them safely:

24 Who, having received such a charge, thrust them into the inner prison, and made their feet fast in the stocks.

25 And at midnight Paul and Silas prayed, and sang praises unto God: and the prisoners heard them.

26 And suddenly there was a great earthquake, so that the foundations of the prison were shaken: and immediately all the doors were opened, and every one's bands were loosed.

27 And the keeper of the prison awaking out of his sleep, and seeing the prison doors open, he drew out his sword, and would have killed himself, supposing that the prisoners had been fled.

Now, Paul and Silas were seasoned disciples who had physically walked with Jesus and received spiritual impartation. But now was time to prove that they paid attention: to apply what they had learned and pass the test.

Paul and Silas were also chosen by God although, not for a specific assignment like Joshua, but to be His disciples.

Matt 28:18-20

18 And Jesus came and spake unto them, saying, All power is given unto me in heaven and in earth.

19 Go ye therefore, and teach all nations, baptizing them in the name of the Father, and of the Son, and of the Holy Ghost:

20 Teaching them to observe all things whatsoever I have commanded you: and, lo, I am with you alway, even unto the end of the world. Amen.

Many times walking with God and doing the things that he has commanded us to do, causes us to suffer persecution, but he has promised to always be with us. Even in these times we can still have peace and joy because we know the God who knows all. And because we have paid attention while in training, during times of hardship our training automatically kicks in. Paul and Silas had an intimate relationship with God. They not only knew his acts but they knew his ways. They knew what it took to tap into the power of God. They knew just what to do to get God's attention, to come to their rescue. Because they knew God and trusted God, so immediately they began to pray and praise Him.

1 John 5:14-15

14 And this is the confidence that we have in him, that, if we ask any thing according to his will, he heareth us:

15 And if we know that he hear us, whatsoever we ask, we know that we have the petitions that we desired of him.

They knew enough about God and his faithfulness that they were beyond faith they were in **Confidence! Now no longer a child of God but Sons/ Daughters of God! T**est, are given to let us know how much we have learned and matured. God already knows. To be entrusted with the things of God we must mature and become sons and daughters.

Gal 4:1-2 Now I say, That the heir, as long as he is a child, differeth nothing from a servant, though he be lord of all; But is under tutors and governors until the time appointed of the father.

What is your response when God is allowing you to be tested? Do you wynn and pout in fear and dismay or do you rejoice and give God praise for what he has already done and is about to manifest?

I remember a time when I was being tested in my finances. God was taking me to another level. I had already passed the test, but didn't expect the process to go the way it did. I had lost my contract after moving into a home where God had instructed me to move. I had purchased furniture from places he had instructed me to. I did everything the way he had revealed it to me, step by step. It was Christmas Eve when I moved in, February I got the knews that in seven days my contract would no longer exist. I said, "O'kay God What's up with this"? Then immediately I thought that I had did all that he had commanded. I went to my dinner table, dressed it with fruit and a bottle of anointed oil that I had prayed over. I said " o'kay God, I did all that you told me. You told me to come here, You told me to go buy all this furniture, You told me to do all that I have done. I was not even trying to go there, but I'm trying to obey you. This was not my plan. This is your baby, If I go down, then you go down, cause I told everybody that you told me to do all this! So here is your bills (and I put all the bills on the table, sumbolic to the one prepared before me in the presence of my enemies). I 'm not gonna freak out and have no fit cause even though I didn't know that my contract was going down you knew before you even told me to come here". These sre my exact words. Why? Because I'm in intimate relationship with Him, and I can be naked and open before him. My bills were almost $1600 a month and my last check after payroll, is 428.00 and everything is due.

Once again God led me to the widow woman and Elijah to sow a seed into the prophets ministry. I had gone there before but this was nothing like $35 dollars, but then again, at that time $35 was about as much a strain as this $320 that He has ordered me to release. God had proven himself faithful, so it was no problem for me to trust him. And he did just what he promised. The barrel was never full, but every time I dipped in it I had what I needed and nothing got cut off, repossessed and I didn't miss a meal. To make a long story short, God had led me to mow my neighbors yard who had been sick with heart trouble. When I did this, I didn't know that I was sowing seed. Then other neighbors wanted me to mow their yards every two weeks.

This was God's way of pushing me into labour to give birth to another entity of my business. Now I am Touch of Anointing Janitorial and Lawn. What the enemy meant for bad, God turn it for my good. But this was the test, after about two months, my clients started backing out one by one. I couldn't see how God was going to do this, it was getting harder and harder. I didn't cut back on my tithes nor my giving, I stayed faithful. I knew it was my tithe and not my seed keeping me alive. Tithe was my level of obedience, but my offerings were my sacrifices and I needed them both, you know like grace and mercy. So just like Peter as I began to focus on the wind, I began to sink, doubt had creeped in. I remember getting my Smokie Norful cd playing the song "I Need You Now", and boo, hooing to God. And as I was down there having my fit, I heard God speak one word, "**wean**". I immediately stopped crying. Then I heard him say, "see that's how babies act when you start trying to wean them". I felt so bad cause I know that my father was grieved because I stopped trusting him. I flunked my test.

That was a Friday, the call came Monday that I had an opportunity to bid on a contract. All the time God was setting me up! The same church where I had started my business, one of the members, William Irby, had gotten the position as plant manager. I met his wife, Terra Irby, who had started her first day of work at the Southern Good Faith Fund where I was attending sessions for my business. I shared with her what I was doing and she informed me that her husband's company was looking for someone to clean their facility. I went the next day for the interview and got the job on the spot because he already knew my level of work. But here's the icing on the cake or the ice cream with the cake. Not only did I have to clean the facility but I also had to keep the lawn. Double for my trouble. But my test prepared me to be in position for the blessing that **He** had for me. God is no respector of person. Now, back to Paul and Silas

Praise not only petitions the hand of God to move on our behalf, but it confuses the enemy. Suddenly the earthquake came to shake the enemies foundation and immediately all doors were opened, and everyone's bands were loosed. When God moves, he deals with every demon that's hindering his work and not one is left to survive in a praise. Your praise is not only for you. Your praise also sets the atmosphere for others to be set free. No demon can stay in the same atmosphere. Praise = Victory.

Isaiah 48:20-49:1 Praise brings forth Redemption

20 Go ye forth of Babylon, flee ye from the Chaldeans, with a voice of singing declare ye, tell this, utter it even to the end of the earth; say ye, The LORD hath redeemed his servant Jacob.

21 And they thirsted not when he led them through the deserts: he caused the waters to flow out of the rock for them: he clave the rock also, and the waters gushed out.

22 There is no peace, saith the LORD, unto the wicked.

He is the God of provision. When God calls you out the way is already made. But there is no peace to the wicked, those who don't come out and those who don't trust God to bring them out. There is no peace when we don't obey.

Ps 32:7-11

7 Thou art my hiding place; thou shalt preserve me from trouble; thou shalt compass me about with songs of deliverance. Selah.

8 I will instruct thee and teach thee in the way in which thou shalt go: I will guide thee with mine eye.

9 Be ye not as the horse, or as the mule, which have no understanding: whose mouth must be held in with bit and bridle, lest they come near unto thee.

10 Many sorrows shall be to the wicked: but he that trusteth in the LORD, mercy shall compass him about.

11 Be glad in the LORD, and rejoice, ye righteous: and shout for joy, all ye that are upright in heart.

Ps 33:8-12

8 Let all the earth fear the LORD: let all the inhabitants of the world stand in awe of him.

9 For he spake, and it was done; he commanded, and it stood fast.

10 The LORD bringeth the counsel of the heathen to nought: he maketh the devices of the people of none effect.

11 The counsel of the LORD standeth forever, the thoughts of his heart to all generations.

12 Blessed is the nation whose God is the LORD: and the people whom he hath chosen for his own inheritance.

Ps 34:4-10

4 I sought the LORD, and he heard me, and delivered me from all my fears.

5 They looked unto him, and were lightened: and their faces were not ashamed.

6 This poor man cried, and the LORD heard him, and saved him out of all his troubles.

7 The angel of the LORD encampeth round about them that fear him, and delivereth them.

8 O taste and see that the LORD is good: blessed is the man that trusteth in him.

9 O fear the LORD, ye his saints: for there is no want to them that fear him.

10 The young lions do lack, and suffer hunger: but they that seek the LORD shall not want any good thing.

Ps 34:15-17

15 The eyes of the LORD are upon the righteous, and his ears are open unto their cry.

16 The face of the LORD is against them that do evil, to cut off the remembrance of them from the earth.

17 The righteous cry, and the LORD heareth, and delivereth them out of all their troubles.

God knows the way, only obey and walk in victory!

Victory is birth out of Peace. Why? Because that's where God Is.

He Knows, But What Do You Know?

Job 23:8-14

8 Behold, I go forward, but he is not there; and backward, but I cannot perceive him:

9 On the left hand, where he doth work, but I cannot behold him: he hideth himself on the right hand, that I cannot see him:

10 But he knoweth the way that I take: when he hath tried me, I shall come forth as gold.

11 My foot hath held his steps, his way have I kept, and not declined.

12 Neither have I gone back from the commandment of his lips; I have esteemed the words of his mouth more than my necessary food.

13 But he is in one mind, and who can turn him? and what his soul desireth, even that he doeth.

14 For he performeth the thing that is appointed for me: and many such things are with him.

Here Job is giving an answer to one of his interrogators, who has suggested to Job that there must be something that he had done, that God has allowed all this to come upon him. And Job here is trying to justify himself when all the time his interrogators are really interrohaters. The thing is that out of all that happened to Job, he didn't curse God and die, he was still standing. All alone in his test, Job didn't quit.

I can only imagine, in the beginning Job was greatly confused, by the suddenness and the intensity of his sufferings. For 7 days and nights he sat with men who claimed to know him, but yet could not find one word to comfort nor encourage him, because all the time they were around, it was to see what they could get. **Beware of Back Stabbers! They smile in your face, all the time wanna to take your place, them back stabbers!**

Because Job's sufferings were so intense (ch3) he began to speak out of his flesh, even cursing the very day that he was born. This was all Satan wanted to hear.

Job 3:25-4:1

25 For the thing which I greatly feared is come upon me, and that which I was afraid of is come unto me.

26 I was **not in safety, neither had I rest, neither was I quiet**; yet trouble came.

Whatever you're going through, Don't trouble your trouble! Job didn't know that he was giving Satan weapons to use against him. **The more he murmured and complained, the more trouble came. When trouble comes you only have two choices, either you're going to stay or you're going to stray, believe and receive, or doubt and run out, Rest or Rebel!**

Matt 11:28-30

28 Come unto me, all ye that labour and are heavy laden, and I will give you rest.

29 Take my yoke upon you, and learn of me; for I am meek and lowly in heart: and ye shall find rest unto your souls.

30 For my yoke is easy, and my burden is light.

When we come to God and don't **Rest** in God, we are in rebellion. It was a command to come and to enter into Rest. Give me your work (yoke) and take my yoke. If you just got to have a yoke upon your neck, let it be the work of God.

Heb 4:1-12

4:1 Let us therefore fear, lest, **a promise being left us** of entering into his rest, any of you should seem to come short of it.

2 For unto us was the gospel preached, as well as unto them: but the word preached did not profit them, not being mixed with faith in them that heard it.

3 For we which have believed do enter into rest, as he said, As I have sworn in my wrath, if they shall enter into my rest: **although the works were finished from the foundation of the world.**

4 For he spake in a certain place of the seventh day on this wise, And God did rest the seventh day from all his works.

5 And in this place again, If they shall enter into my rest.

6 Seeing therefore it remaineth that some must enter therein, and they to whom it was first preached entered not in because of unbelief:

7 Again, he limiteth a certain day, saying in David, To day, after so long a time; as it is said, To day if ye will hear his voice, harden not your hearts.

8 For if Jesus had given them rest, then would he not afterward have spoken of another day.

9 There remaineth therefore a rest to the people of God.

10 For he that is entered into his rest, he also hath **ceased from his own works,** as God did from his.

11 Let us labour therefore to enter into that rest, lest any man fall after the same example of unbelief.

12 For the word of God is quick, and powerful, and sharper than any twoedged sword, piercing even to the dividing asunder of soul and spirit, and of the joints and marrow, and is a discerner of the thoughts and intents of the heart.

To Rest in God means to cease from our own works (what we think is right). And because those before us did not mix with faith, they died in the wilderness. They never made it to the promise land, because they found no Rest (they murmured and complained). God did not cause Job all his grief, Job did. **God allowed the TEST, but it was up to Job to know and speak the right answer. And because of his fear, he received his faith!** Because of his FEAR he was not in SAFETY, he didn't find REST, and he didn't SHUT HIS MOUTH.

Isa 30:15

15 For thus saith the Lord GOD, the Holy One of Israel; In returning and **rest** shall ye be saved; in **quietness and in confidence** shall be your strength: and ye would not. To find REST is to find PEACE.

But in chapter 23 Job had a **shift in his spirit.**

8 Behold, I go forward, but he is not there; and backward, but I cannot perceive him:

9 On the left hand, where he doth work, but I cannot behold him: he hideth himself on the right hand, that I cannot see him:

10 But he knoweth the way that I take: when he hath tried me, I shall come forth as gold.

Job said although I can't see him, and don't know where he is, I don't fully understand, **But one thing I know, He knows the way that I take.**

Jeremiah 29: 11 For I know the plans that I have for you declares the Lord, plans to prosper you and not to harm you, plans to give you a future and a hope.

Matthew 13:11 It is given unto you to know the mystery (plan) of the Kingdom

Some say that God works in mysterious ways, but when we have a true relationship, built on trust and obedience, God won't leave us in the dark. God will impregnate us with his plan. The problem is we can't get pregnant with just foreplay. Some of us want to play with God and he's not having it. He's not having illegitimate babies, so if we don't agree to come to the mariage, there can be no intimacy.

When the shift came, Job's was able to renew his focus and suddenly he realized. **It's Only A Test!** Job now began to shift again.

11 My foot hath held his steps, his way have I kept, and not declined.

(encouraged himself)

12 Neither have I gone back from the commandment of his lips; I have esteemed the words of his mouth more than my necessary food.

13 But he is in one mind, and who can turn him? and what his soul desireth, even that he doeth. (what God's is set, who change it; whatever he wills, that's what it will be)

14 For he performeth the thing that is **appointed** for me: and many such things are with him.

Job realized that who he was looking for, he was looking in all the wrong places, and what he needed to know was already in him. **Your answer is already in you.**

2 Peter 1:3

According as his divine power hath given unto us all things that pertain unto life and godliness, through the knowledge of him that hath called us to glory and virtue:

At midnight Job's alarm went off, **It's Only A Test!** And if it's a test, then that means you already know the answer. God won't test you if He hasn't already prepared you. What you got to do is go back to school and let your training kick in. The same word that brought you to the test, is the same word that will enable you to pass the test. **The Answer Stayed The Same!** Go back to the word. When you can't track his hand, trust his plan. God knows what he's doing and he's not going to change his mind. God is performing a thing that is appointed unto you, but your time has not come.

Hab 2:3

For the vision is yet for an appointed time, but at the end it shall speak, and not lie: though it tarry, wait for it; because it will surely come, it will not tarry

Rebellion or Rest

The Rejected Promise
Matthew 11:28; Hebrew 4: all

Rest - Is freedom from activity or labor; peace of mind or spirit; to take relief from.

Labor- hard work, to act or move with difficulty.

Labour - To bring forth, to give birth to.

The greatest promise made apart from salvation and eternal life falls in between and that is **Rest**. It is our rest that allows us to enter into eternal life. The Bible often speaks of the rest of God. Many times pertaining to the Sabbath.

Ex 23:12

"Six days thou shalt do thy work, and on the seventh day thou shalt rest: that thine ox and thine ass may rest, and the son of thy handmaid, and the stranger, may be refreshed." There is a rest that God has ordained for everyday living, not limited to one day. This one day, was only a schoolmaster, a token of what was to come; teaching us how we are to conduct ourselves in everyday living!

Gal 3:22-26

22 But the scripture hath concluded all under sin, that the promise by faith of Jesus Christ might be given to them that believe.

23 But before faith came, we were kept under the law, shut up unto the faith which should afterwards be revealed.

24 Wherefore the law was our schoolmaster to bring us unto Christ, that we might be justified by faith.

25 But after that faith is come, we are no longer under a schoolmaster.

26 For ye are all the children of God by faith in Christ Jesus.

I Chronicles 22:9 Solomon was a man of Rest, who operated in the infinite wisdom of God (His word), a man of confidence, not worry.

"Behold, a son shall be born to thee, who shall be a man of rest; and I will give him rest from all his enemies round about: for his name shall be Solomon, and I will give peace and quietness unto Israel in his days".

Job 3:17-26

17 There the wicked cease from troubling; and there the weary be at rest.

18 There the prisoners rest together; they hear not the voice of the oppressor.

19 The small and great are there; and the servant is free from his master.

20 Wherefore is light given to him that is in misery, and life unto the bitter in soul;

21 Which long for death, but it cometh not; and dig for it more than for hid treasures;

22 Which rejoice exceedingly, and are glad, when they can find the grave?

23 Why is light given to a man whose way is hid, and whom God hath hedged in?

24 For my sighing cometh before I eat, and my roarings are poured out like the waters.

25 For the thing which I greatly feared is come upon me, and that which I was afraid of is come unto me.

26 I was not in safety, neither had I rest, Job speaks of a place of eternal Rest, apart from everyday troubles. It was Job's attitude that kept him from the place of rest. Dwelling on his present state. Job's refusal to enter into rest brought great destruction upon him. Because he murmured and complained, 24) sighing, not thankful and ungrateful, 25) fear took the

place of rest and opened the door for demonic attacks. 26) Rest is a place of safety that Job did not enter. And because he was not quiet, the things that he spoke (feared) came upon him. **Do not speak your fears. Satan responds to fear like God responds to faith. What we speak out of our mouth is what our actions will line up with. So when we respond to fear, we set in motion things to cause that very thing we fear to come to past; by giving that seed of fear a womb for reproduction and birth. Just like faith, when we respond to faith, it sets in motion things that will cause what we believe to come to past. So my actions let me know truly what I believe. So when I act upon what I fear, it's what I believe to be true, it is what I'm pregnant with and that's what I will have.**

Isaiah 30:15

For thus saith the Lord GOD, the Holy One of Israel; In returning and rest shall ye be saved; in quietness and in confidence shall be your strength: and ye would not. **Rebellion instead of Rest!**

Jeremiah 6:16

Thus saith the LORD, Stand ye in the ways, and see, and ask for the old paths, where is the good way, and walk therein, and ye shall find rest for your souls. But they said, We will not walk therein. God gave a command to seek guidance for his way, which is the only way which leads to Rest. But Israel said, " We will not walk therein"! **Rebellion instead of Rest!**

Psalms 62:1

Truly my soul waiteth upon God: from him cometh my salvation.

Rest only comes from God, (His Word) **John 1:1** In the beginning was the Word, and the Word was with God, and the Word was God.

Psalms 91:1

91:1 He that dwelleth in the secret place of the most High shall abide under the shadow of the Almighty.

2 I will say of the LORD, He is my refuge and my fortress: my God; in him will I trust.

3 Surely he shall deliver thee from the snare of the fowler, and from the noisome pestilence.

4 He shall cover thee with his feathers, and under his wings shalt thou trust: his truth shall be thy shield and buckler.

5 Thou shalt not be afraid for the terror by night; nor for the arrow that flieth by day;

6 Nor for the pestilence that walketh in darkness; nor for the destruction that wasteth at noonday.

7 A thousand shall fall at thy side, and ten thousand at thy right hand; but it shall not come nigh thee.

8 Only with thine eyes shalt thou behold and see the reward of the wicked.

9 Because thou hast made the LORD, which is my refuge, even the most High, thy habitation;

10 There shall no evil befall thee, neither shall any plague come nigh thy dwelling.

11 For he shall give his angels charge over thee, to keep thee in all thy ways.

12 They shall bear thee up in their hands, lest thou dash thy foot against a stone.

13 Thou shalt tread upon the lion and adder: the young lion and the dragon shalt thou trample under feet.

14 Because he hath set his love upon me, therefore will I deliver him: I will set him on high, because he hath known my name.

15 He shall call upon me, and I will answer him: I will be with him in trouble; I will deliver him, and honour him.

16 With long life will I satisfy him, and shew him my salvation.

When we learn to rest in God, everything that we need is given by divine intervention. All according to his divine will, (time)

2 Peter 1:3-4

3 **According** as his divine power hath given unto us all things that pertain unto life and godliness, through the knowledge of him that hath called us to glory and virtue:

4 Whereby are given unto us exceeding great and precious promises: that by these ye might be partakers of the divine nature, having escaped the corruption that is in the world through lust. **Oneness, in unity with the Father.**

He that dwelleth, abideth (Rest) in the secret place, shall abide (Rest) under the shadow of the almighty God. The word is our covering and should not be placed under our feet (we do not stand on the promises), this place is where the enemy belongs. We are to rest in his word, (relax, chill). Without rest our hearts are hardened, which leads to rebellion and puts us in the way of God's wrath. **Ps 95:11** Unto whom I sware in my wrath that they should not enter into my rest. God commands us to rest.

Isaiah 11:10

And in that day there shall be a root of Jesse, which shall stand for an ensign of the people; to it shall the Gentiles seek: and his rest shall be glorious. The prophecy of Christ and the glory of his rest; Rest brings glory to the father. There is no other way to God's glory, it only comes through rest.

Revelation 14: 11-13

11 And the smoke of their torment ascendeth up for ever and ever: and they have no rest day nor night, who worship the beast and his image, and whosoever receiveth the mark of his name.

12 Here is the patience of the saints: here are they that keep the commandments of God, and the faith of Jesus.

13 And I heard a voice from heaven saying unto me, Write, Blessed are the dead which die in the Lord from henceforth: Yea, saith the Spirit, that they may rest from their labours; and their works do follow them.

The rebellious must suffer the eternal torment. **No Rest, No worship; No Worship, No Rain!** But they that die in the Lord, that keep the commandments of God (Rested), and the faith of Jesus (Rest), yea saith the Spirit, that they may REST from their labours; and their works do follow them.(eternal reward)

REST
Hebrew 4: 1-16

1 Let us therefore fear,**(reverence)** lest, a promise being left us **(belonging to, inherited, due, owed, set aside for)** of entering into his rest, any of you should seem to come short of it. Matt 11:28 "Come unto me, all ye that labour and are heavy laden, and I will give you rest". The promise is the Rest of God

2 For unto us was the gospel preached, as well as unto them: but the word preached did not profit them,**(to be of use or advantage, to somebody or something)** not being mixed with faith in them that heard it.

3 For we which have believed do enter into rest, as he said, As I have sworn in my wrath, if they shall enter into my rest: **although the works were finished from the foundation of the world.** Matt 22:4 Again, he sent forth other servants, saying, Tell them which are bidden, Behold, I have prepared my dinner: my oxen and my fatlings are killed, and **all** things are ready: **come** unto the marriage. Everything that we will ever need, every promise has already been fulfilled, from the time of creation. It is settled, in the warehouse of heaven, reserved for us; in God's appointed time.

Ps 119:89

For ever, O LORD, thy word is settled in heaven. **1 Peter 1:4-5** To an inheritance incorruptible, and undefiled, and that fadeth not away, reserved in heaven for you, Who are kept by the power of God through faith unto salvation **ready** to be revealed **in** the last **time. Mal 3:11** And I will rebuke the devourer for your sakes, and he shall not destroy the fruits of your ground; neither shall your **vine** cast her fruit before the **time** in the field, saith the LORD of hosts. **John 15:5** I am the **vine,** ye are the branches: He that abideth **(REST)** in me, and I **(REST)** in him, the same bringeth forth much fruit: for without me ye can do nothing. Our job is to REST in the word,(become one with), to bring heaven here on earth. **Matt 6:10** Thy kingdom come. Thy will be done **in** earth, **as** it is **in** heaven.

4 For he spake in a certain place of the seventh day on this wise, And God did rest the seventh day from all his works. When God rested, his works were finished.

5 And in **this (What place? Where God is, in his presence. A place of intimacy, where we believe and conceive to become pregnant)** place again, If they shall enter into my rest.

6 Seeing therefore, it remaineth that some must enter therein, and they to whom it was first preached entered not in because of unbelief:

7 Again, he limiteth a certain day, saying in David, To day, after so long a time; as it is said, To day if ye will hear his voice, harden not your hearts.

8 For **if** Jesus had given them rest,**(we must receive)** then would he not afterward have spoken of another day.

9 There remaineth therefore a rest to the people of God.

There still remains because we don't believe. Be not conformed to this world **Rom. 12:2!** The reason we see so much of the world on the church is because we are afraid of true intimacy. We are spiritual virgins and have not allowed the Holy Spirit to have his way in us. And because he is gentle, he will not force himself on us. (get the revelation)

10 For he that is entered into his rest, he also hath ceased from his own works, as God did from his. When we rest, our struggle is over. The struggle was our trying to do it in our own time, strength and power, becoming entangled, not pleasing God. **2 Tim 2:4** No man that warreth entangleth himself with the affairs of this life; that he may please him who hath chosen him to be a soldier.

11 Let us labour (bring forth, give birth to) therefore to enter into that rest, lest any man fall after the same example of unbelief. (Why?)

12 For the word of God is quick, and powerful, and sharper than any two-edged sword, piercing even to the dividing asunder of soul and spirit, and of the joints and marrow, and is a discerner of the thoughts and intents of the heart.

13 Neither is there any creature that is not manifest in his sight: but all things are naked and opened unto the eyes of him with whom we have to do. The word is all in all and nothing can hide from the word.

14 Seeing then that we have a great high priest, the best above all, that is passed into the heavens, Jesus passed the rest test, Jesus the Son of God, let us hold fast our profession, what we declare righteous and just.

15 For we have not an high priest which cannot be touched with the feeling of our infirmities; but was in all points tempted like as we are, yet without sin. He knows our struggles and our emotions and can relate to them, though He too, was tempted (tested, proven) ye without sin

16 Let us therefore come boldly unto the throne of grace, that we may obtain mercy, and find grace to help in time of need. So let noting hold you back, not even sin. Come boldly when we mess up He knows how we feel, but come to receive grace. Come boldly, not with the feeling of your infirmity (guilt). For if we do, we will not touch God, because of our guilt (condemnation). I John 3:20-22 For if our heart condemn us, God is greater than our heart, and knoweth all things. Beloved, if our heart condemn us not, then have we confidence toward God. And whatsoever we ask, we receive of him, because we keep his commandments, and do

those things that are pleasing in his sight. **We must cleanse ourselves with the word and then come, boldly!**

Angels,
Ministering Spirits

Heb 1:14-2:1

14 Are they not all ministering spirits, sent forth to minister for them who shall be heirs of salvation? Angels are God's agents, who go about establishing God's covenant. They are the one's responsible for the will of God being brought to pass in our lives, going about setting things in motion as we confess and do God's word. Giving God pleasure and glory.

Ps 103:20-21 Bless the LORD, ye his angels, that excel in strength, that do his commandments, hearkening unto the voice of his word. Bless ye the LORD, all ye his hosts; ye ministers of his, that do his pleasure. God's pleasure could be His blessing or His wrath. Ps 104:4 Who maketh his angels spirits; his ministers a flaming fire: Ps 35:5-6 Let them be as chaff before the wind: and let the angel of the LORD chase them. Let their way be dark and slippery: and let the angel of the LORD persecute them.

Hindrances to Entering
The Rest of God

Unbelief, Heb 4: 3 For, we which have believed do enter into rest, as he said, As I have sworn in my wrath, if they shall enter into my rest: although the works were finished from the foundation of the world. We must be properly planted to flourish. Not to preserve the religious heritage of our parents, but to be in the presence of the un-compromised word of faith. It's a good idea for those who are just starting out to go to the church closest to where you live. But at some point and time we must allow God to direct us, and plant us where He wants us. If it takes 3 hours to get there one way, it's worth it to be in the will of God. The place where you can prosper spiritually and naturally.

Disobedience, Heb 3:12; 4:11 Take heed, brethren, lest there be in any of you an evil heart of unbelief, in departing from the living God. Heb4:11 Let us labour therefore to enter into that rest, lest any man fall after the same example of unbelief. Unbelief brings disobedience, which causes us to walk away from the will of God, which results in us falling into sin. Obedience is a way of measuring our faith. The more we believe the more we will do.

Lack of Action James 2:17 Even so faith, if it hath not works, is dead, being alone.

Hardened Hearts Heb 3:15-17 While it is said, To day if ye will hear his voice, harden not your hearts, as in the provocation. For some, when they had heard, did provoke (harden) not all that came out of Egypt by Moses. But with whom was he grieved forty years? Was it not with them that had sinned (hardened their hearts) whose carcases fell in the wilderness? A hardened heart brings about rebellion, which keeps wandering in or even dying the wilderness. Either way, we do not enter into the place of promise that comes through obeying the word of God.

Spiritual Slothfulness, Lazy Rom 1:17 For therein is the righteousness of God revealed from faith to faith: as it is written, The just shall live by faith. Unbelief, disobedience, lack of action, hardened hearts all contribute in stopping spiritual maturity, which results in slowing our **growth.**

Issues of the soul (feel, think chooser) controled by emotions

Wrong thinking Ps 19:14 Let the words of my mouth and the meditation of my heart Be acceptable in Your sight, O LORD, my rock and my Redeemer. The must be an agreement of our mouth and heart. Not just mere words. Our thinking must be in line with God's word. We must submerge ourselves in the word of God. Overdose; to change your minds we must be brain washed. Wrong thinking will hinder from possessing the promised land.

Lack of Courage Josh 1:9 Have not I commanded thee? Be strong and of a good courage; be not afraid, neither be thou dismayed: for the LORD thy God is with thee whithersoever thou goest. We must have courage to step out in faith. Courage is not the absence of fear; having **courage is the strength to act upon God's word in the presence of fear. Doing what the word says even when fear is there. Do it afraid. Fear is a spirit that comes to stop you. But courage walks over fear, courage does not stop but proceeds forth. Like a linebacker, courage runs over fear and blocks, so that I, the wide receiver can make the catch and run a touchdown! 2 Tim 1:7** For God hath **not** given us the spirit of fear; but of power,(HolySpirit) and of love,(Father) and of a sound mind (Son). **The three line backers.**

Kingdom Builders
Psalms 127:1

Except the Lord build the house, they labour in vain that build it; Except the Lord keep the city the watchman waketh in but in vain.

Being confident of this very thing, that he who hath begun a good work in you will perform it until the day of Jesus Christ. **Phil. 1:6**

God has to be the author and the finisher. God is not obligated to finish what he did not author. Anything that God did not author is an Ishmael **(wrong vision)**. Anything that God did not finish is an Ishmael **(right vision, wrong time)**.

Rom 9:4-9

4 Who are Israelites; to whom pertaineth the adoption, and the glory, and the covenants, and the giving of the law, and the service of God, and the promises;

5 Whose are the fathers, and of whom as concerning the flesh Christ came, who is over all, God blessed for ever. Amen.

6 Not as though the word of God hath taken none effect. For they are not all Israel, which are of Israel:

7 Neither, because they are the seed of Abraham, are they all children: but, In Isaac shall thy seed be called.

8 That is, They which are the children of the flesh, these are not the children of God: but the children of the promise are counted for the seed.

9 For this is the word of promise, At this time will I come, and Sara shall have a son.

God can not bring the promise of the blessing upon an Ishmael of any sort. Why?

1 Cor 1:29

That no flesh should glory in his presence.

Isa 42:8

I am the LORD: that is my name: and my glory will I not give to another, neither my praise to graven images.

Isa 48:11

For mine own sake, even for mine own sake, will I do it: for how should my name be polluted? and I will not give my glory unto another.

The blessing can only come through the promise.

Gal 4:22-5:1

5 For it is written, that Abraham had two sons, the one by a bondmaid, the other by a freewoman.

6 But he who was of the bondwoman was born after the flesh; but he of the freewoman was by promise.

7 Which things are an allegory: for these are the two covenants; the one from the mount Sinai, which gendereth to bondage, which is Agar.

8 For this Agar is mount Sinai in Arabia, and answereth to Jerusalem which now is, and is in bondage with her children.

9 But Jerusalem which is above is free, which is the mother of us all.

10 For it is written, Rejoice, thou barren that bearest not; break forth and cry, thou that travailest not: for the desolate hath many more children than she which hath an husband.

11 Now we, brethren, as Isaac was, are the children of promise.

12 But as then he that was born after the flesh persecuted him that was born after the Spirit, even so it is now.

13 Nevertheless what saith the scripture? Cast out the bondwoman and her son: for the son of the bondwoman shall not be heir with the son of the free woman.

14 So then, brethren, we are not children of the bondwoman, but of the free.

Bond woman = mans way, Flesh (the world's way)

Free Woman = God's way, word (led of the Spirit)

Prov 10:22

The blessing of the LORD, it maketh rich, and he addeth no sorrow with it.

Nevertheless what saith the scripture? Cast out the bondwoman and her son: for the son of the bondwoman shall not be heir with the son of the free woman. **Whatever is birthed out o our flesh, that God did not author, eventually has to die or will be required as seed. Mark 10:29-30**

29 And Jesus answered and said, Verily I say unto you, There is no man that hath left house, or brethren, or sisters, or father, or mother, or wife, or children, or lands, for my sake, and the gospel's,

30 But he shall receive an hundredfold now in this time, houses, and brethren, and sisters, and mothers, and children, and lands, with persecutions; and in the world to come eternal life. **Ishmael can not inherit the promise, flesh can not inherit the Kingdom of God. 1 Cor 15:50**

Now this I say, brethren, flesh and blood cannot inherit the kingdom of God; neither doth corruption inherit incorruption. **The kingdom of God is God's way of doing things, birthed out of the word, promise = Spirit.**

Prov 3:5-6

5 Trust in the LORD with all thine heart; and lean not unto thine own understanding.

6 In all thy ways acknowledge him, and he shall direct thy paths.

Luke 5:8

When Simon Peter saw it, he fell down at Jesus' knees, saying, Depart from me; for I am a sinful man, O Lord.

Peter was sinful because he didn't acknowledge Him (Jesus) and do it His way from the beginning. We must die to our will and way.

John 12:24-26

24 Verily, verily, I say unto you, Except a corn of wheat fall into the ground and die, it abideth alone: but if it die, it bringeth forth much fruit.

25 He that loveth his life shall lose it; and he that hateth his life in this world shall keep it unto life eternal.

26 If any man serve me, let him follow me; and where I am, there shall also my servant be: if any man serve me, him will my Father honour. **We must die to multiply. We must allow God to plant us an Holy seed, then REST= where germination takes place.**

1 Cor 15:34-50

34 Awake to righteousness, and sin not; for some have not the knowledge of God: I speak this to your shame.

35 But some man will say, How are the dead raised up? and with what body do they come?

36 Thou fool, that which thou sowest is not quickened, except it die:

37 And that which thou sowest, thou sowest not that body that shall be, but bare grain, it may chance of wheat, or of some other grain:

38 But God giveth it a body (glory) as it hath pleased him, and to every seed his own body.

39 All flesh is not the same flesh: but there is one kind of flesh of men, another flesh of beasts, another of fishes, and another of birds.

40 There are also celestial bodies, and bodies terrestrial: but the glory of the celestial is one, and the glory of the terrestrial is another.

41 There is one glory of the sun, and another glory of the moon, and another glory of the stars: for one star differeth from another star in glory.

42 So also is the resurrection of the dead. It is sown in corruption; it is raised in incorruption:

43 It is sown in dishonour; it is raised in glory: it is sown in weakness; it is raised in power:

44 It is sown a natural body; it is raised a spiritual body. There is a natural body, and there is a spiritual body.

45 And so it is written, The first man Adam was made a living soul; the last Adam was made a quickening spirit.

46 Howbeit that was not first which is spiritual, but that which is natural; and afterward that which is spiritual.

47 The first man is of the earth, earthy: the second man is the Lord from heaven.

48 As is the earthy, such are they also that are earthy: and as is the heavenly, such are they also that are heavenly.

49 And as we have borne the image of the earthy, we shall also bear the image of the heavenly.

50 Now this I say, brethren, that flesh and blood cannot inherit the kingdom of God; neither doth corruption inherit incorruption.

The process of Death
2 Cor 5:15-17

And that he died for all, that they which live, should not henceforth live unto themselves, but unto him which died for them, and rose again.

Wherefore henceforth know we no man after the flesh: yea, though we have known Christ after the flesh, yet now henceforth know we him no more.

Therefore if any man be in Christ, he is a new creature: old things are passed away; behold, all things are become new.

The new man is born of the spirit, through the process of a renewed mind. Rom 12:1-2

I beseech you therefore, brethren, by the mercies of God, that ye present your bodies a living sacrifice, holy, acceptable unto God, which is your reasonable service.

And be not conformed to this world: but be ye transformed by the renewing of your mind, that ye may prove what is that good, and acceptable, and perfect, will of God.

1 Peter 1:3-7

3 Blessed be the God and Father of our Lord Jesus Christ, which according to his abundant mercy hath begotten us again unto a lively hope by the resurrection of Jesus Christ from the dead,

4 To an **inheritance** incorruptible, and undefiled, and that fadeth not away, **reserved in heaven** for you, (**Ps 119:89**

For ever, O LORD, thy word is settled in heaven.) Our inheritance is the word of God.

5 Who are **kept** by the power of God through faith unto salvation ready to be revealed in the last time. **The word will keep you in all areas until the promise is manifested.**

6 Wherein ye greatly rejoice, though now for a season, if need be, ye are in heaviness through manifold temptations:

7 That the **trial** of your faith, being much more precious than of gold that perisheth, though it be **tried with fire**, might be found unto praise and honour and glory at the appearing of Jesus Christ: **The trial of fire prepares you to receive, purifying the heart and motive. The place of death, the grave is the place of REST= the place of unity.**

Ps 23:3-4

He restoreth my soul: he leadeth me in the paths of righteousness for his name's sake.

Yea, though I walk through the valley of the **shadow of death**, I will fear no evil: for thou art with me; thy rod and thy staff they comfort me. **The place of restored unity, fellowship, worship, oneness. The cross was a place of death/life. Restored my soul** (will); **Restore: Bring back to original condition or place.**

John 17:5

And now, O Father, glorify thou me with thine own self with the glory **which I had with thee before the world was.** Not born of the will of the flesh, but the will of God. **The valley is the cross, it's not what it looks like; where the shadow of death produces life.**

Heb 4:3

For we which have believed do enter into rest, as he said, As I have sworn in my wrath, if they shall enter into my rest: **although the works were finished from the foundation of the world.** Already done, reserved in heaven, for God's appointed time.

Heb 4:10-13

10 For he that is entered into his rest, he also hath ceased from his own works, as God did from his.

11 Let us labour therefore to enter into that rest, lest any man fall after the same example of unbelief.

12 For the word of God is quick, and powerful, and sharper than any twoedged sword, piercing even to the dividing asunder of soul and spirit, and of the joints and marrow, and is a discerner of the thoughts and intents of the heart.

13 Neither is there any creature that is not manifest in his sight: but all things are naked and opened unto the eyes of him with whom we have to do. **God's resume' is assured with a guarantee.**

Heb 3:1-14

1 Wherefore, holy brethren, partakers of the heavenly calling, consider the Apostle and High Priest of our profession, Christ Jesus;

2 Who was faithful to him that appointed him, as also Moses was faithful in all his house. **Old way, old covenant, flesh**

3 For this man was counted worthy of more glory than Moses, inasmuch as he who hath builded the house hath more honour than the house. **Christ, new way, new covenant, Spirit**

4 For every house is builded by some man; but he that built all things is God. **(Psalms 127:1)**

5 And Moses verily was faithful in all his house, as a servant, for a testimony of those things which **were to be** spoken after; **old, bondage, servant = set up for future glory**

6 But Christ as a son over his own house; whose house are we, if we hold fast the confidence and the rejoicing of the hope firm unto the end. **New, liberty, friend = promise**

7 Wherefore (as the Holy Ghost saith, To day if ye will hear his voice, **Don't grieve the Spirit of God**

8 Harden not your hearts, as in the provocation, in the day of temptation in the wilderness:

9 When your fathers tempted me, proved me, and saw my works forty years.

10 Wherefore I was grieved with that generation, and said, They do alway err in their heart; and they have not known my ways. **They did not know God's ways, only knew his acts. Without the word and obedience we can not become one (intimate) with God to truly get to know him.**

11 So I sware in my wrath, They shall not enter into my rest.)

12 Take heed, brethren, lest there be in any of you an evil heart of unbelief, in departing from the living God.

13 But exhort one another daily, while it is called To day; lest any of you be hardened through the deceitfulness of sin. **A hardened heart is one that is not willing to let go and let God when He calls.**

14 For we are made partakers of Christ, if we hold the beginning of our confidence stedfast unto the end; **We can have the same glory, partakers of Christ glory, if we submit to His voice when He calls.**

In The Waiting
A Place of Servanthood
Isaiah 40:31

But those who wait on the LORD shall renew their strength;

They shall mount up with wings like eagles, they shall run and not be weary, they shall walk and not faint.

Those that wait for Him-seek Godly counsel, trust in God, minister unto God, expect of God, hope in God, labour with God, Positioned in God and rest in/with God, crucify the flesh (**DIE**) shall renew their strength. **These are all prerequisites to abiding in God, that places us in position to receive from God.**

For – As showing favor to (Him)**, on behalf of** (Him)**; doing His will.**

For we are his workmanship, created in Christ Jesus unto good works, which God hath before ordained that we should walk in them. **Eph 2:10-11**

Isa 30:18

And therefore will **the LORD wait**, that he may be gracious unto you, and therefore will he be exalted, that he may have mercy upon you: for the LORD is a God of judgment: blessed are all they that wait for him. **God does not require anything of us that He himself does not do. He's waiting, in position, for us. A place of expectancy!**

Ps 40:1

I waited patiently for the LORD; and he inclined unto me, and heard my cry.

Waiting patiently for, (not just sit and expect). Laboured patiently – when given orders, Rested patiently – not murmuring and complaining

Run and not be weary, walk and not faint. This means constant movement making progress.

Ps 37:34

Wait **on** the LORD, and keep his way, and he shall exalt thee to inherit the land: when the wicked are cut off, thou shalt see it. **Let God lead, don't get ahead of Him. It's all in his timing! keep His way, keep His word**

Ps 119:130

he entrance of thy words giveth light; it giveth understanding unto the simple.

Ps 119:105

Thy word is a lamp unto my feet, and a light unto my path

God's word gives light, Understanding! Who, what, when, where, why, which, how, how many. The word answers all.

Ps 37:3-7

3 Trust in the LORD and do good; so shalt thy dwell in the land and verily thou shall be fed.

4 **Delight** thyself also in the LORD; and he shall give thee the desires of thine heart.

5 **Commit** thy way to the LORD; trust also in him and shall bring it to pass.

6 He will make your righteousness as the light, and thy judgement as the noonday.

7 **Rest** in the LORD and wait patiently for him; fret not thyself because of him who prospereth in his way, because of man who bringeth wicked devises to pass.

Ps 27:14

Wait on the LORD; Be of good courage, And He shall strengthen your heart; Wait, I say, on the LORD! **If we are faithful to do our part, God is faithful to do his part.**

A Temporary Change of Address
**Sorry to disappoint you, But my address has changed.
It ain't what it looks like!**

John 15: 14-23 The servant is not above his Lord.

14 Ye are my friends, if ye do whatsoever I command you.

15 Henceforth I call you not servants; for the servant knoweth not what his lord doeth: but I have called you friends; for all things that I have heard of my Father I have made known unto you.

16 Ye have not chosen me, but I have chosen you, and ordained you, that ye should go and bring forth fruit, and that your fruit should remain: that whatsoever ye shall ask of the Father in my name, he may give it you.

17 These things I command you, that ye love one another.

18 If the world hate you, ye know that it hated me before it hated you.

19 If ye were of the world, the world would love his own: but because ye are not of the world, but I have chosen you out of the world, therefore the world hateth you.

20 Remember the word that I said unto you, The servant is not greater than his lord. If they have persecuted me, they will also persecute you; if they have kept my saying, they will keep yours also.

21 But all these things will they do unto you for my name's sake, because they know not him that sent me.

22 If I had not come and spoken unto them, they had not had sin: but now they have no cloke for their sin.

23 He that hateth me hateth my Father also.

John 16:1-4 Remember, God is with in the beginning.

1 These things have I spoken unto you, that ye should not be offended.

2 They shall put you out of the synagogues: yea, the time cometh, that whosoever killeth you will think that he doeth God service.

3 And these things will they do unto you, because they have not known the Father, nor me.

4 But these things have I told you, that when the time shall come, ye may remember that I told you of them. And these things I said not unto you at the beginning, because I was with you.

Matt. 10: 16-24 God sends you forth, great the betrayal, for His glory.

16 Behold, I send you forth as sheep in the midst of wolves: be ye therefore wise as serpents, and harmless as doves.

17 But beware of men: for they will deliver you up to the councils, and they will scourge you in their synagogues;

18 And ye shall be brought before governors and kings for my sake, for a testimony against them and the Gentiles.

19 But when they deliver you up, take no thought how or what ye shall speak: for it shall be given you in that same hour what ye shall speak.

20 For it is not ye that speak, but the Spirit of your Father which speaketh in you.

21 And the brother shall deliver up the brother to death, and the father the child: and the children shall rise up against their parents, and cause them to be put to death.

22 And ye shall be hated of all men for my name's sake: but he that endureth to the end shall be saved.

23 But when they persecute you in this city, flee ye into another: for verily I say unto you, Ye shall not have gone over the cities of Israel, till the Son of man be come.

24 The disciple is not above his master, nor the servant above his lord.

Isaiah 54:14-17 Righteousness destroys every weapon.

14 In righteousness shalt thou be established: thou shalt be far from oppression; for thou shalt not fear: and from terror; for it shall not come near thee.

15 Behold, they shall surely gather together, but not by me: whosoever shall gather together against thee shall fall for thy sake.

16 Behold, I have created the smith that bloweth the coals in the fire, and that bringeth forth an instrument for his work; and I have created the waster to destroy.

17 **No weapon** that is formed against thee shall prosper; and every tongue that shall rise against thee in judgment thou shalt condemn. This is the heritage of the servants of the LORD, and their **righteousness** is of me, saith the LORD.

Proverb 12: 28 God's way brings life.

In the way of **righteousness** is life; and in the pathway thereof there is **no death.**

We Don't Die, We Multiply!

Isaiah 55:8-13 The ways of God, His Word! *13 Instead of

8 For my thoughts are not your thoughts, neither are your ways my ways, saith the LORD.

9 For as the heavens are higher than the earth, so are my ways higher than your ways, and my thoughts than your thoughts.

10 For as the rain cometh down, and the snow from heaven, and returneth not thither, but watereth the earth, and maketh it bring forth and bud, that it may give seed to the sower, and bread to the eater:

11 So shall my word be that goeth forth out of my mouth: it shall not return unto me void, but it shall accomplish that which I please, and it shall prosper in the thing whereto I sent it.

12 For ye shall go out with joy, and be led forth with peace: the mountains and the hills shall break forth before you into singing, and all the trees of the field shall clap their hands.

13 Instead of the thorn shall come up the fir tree, and instead of the brier shall come up the myrtle tree: and it shall be to the LORD for a name, for an **everlasting sign** that shall not be cut off.

The word of God brings change. Instead of what it looks like, God's word makes, (transforms) it into what His word says it should be. It is an everlasting sign that shall not be cut off, because it has been established **(rooted, grounded)** in Righteousness (**according to the will of God**), His **Covenant!**

God's Covenant is established through Angel Power.

Ps. 103:20-21

Bless the LORD, ye his angels, that excel in strength, that **do his commandment**s, hearkening unto the voice of **his word**.

Bless ye the LORD, all ye his hosts; ye ministers of his, **that do his pleasure.**(his will)

Ps. 105: 8-10 Ps 105:8-10

8 He hath remembered **his covenant** for ever, **the word which he commanded** to a thousand generations.

9 Which covenant he made with Abraham, and his oath unto Isaac;

10 And confirmed the same unto Jacob for a law, and to Israel for an **everlasting covenant:**

Heb. 1: 13-14

But to which of the angels said he at any time, Sit on my right hand, until I make thine enemies thy footstool?

Are they not all, ministering spirits, sent forth **to minister** for them who shall be **heirs** of salvation? Angels are sent forth to meet the needs of those who are trusting God for their rightful inheritance, His Word! They are the workers of God's warehouse; filling orders and transporting His Kingdom from heaven to earth.

Now let's look at some faithful witnesses.

The Master
Matt. 27: 62 - 28: 13
*64 The Angel came by night

62 Now the next day, that followed the day of the preparation, the chief priests and Pharisees came together unto Pilate,

63 Saying, Sir, we remember that that deceiver said, while he was yet alive, After three days I will rise again.

64 Command therefore that the sepulchre be made sure until the third day, lest his disciples come by night, and steal him away, and say unto the

people, He is risen from the dead: so the last error shall be worse than the first.

65 Pilate said unto them, Ye have a watch: go your way, make it as sure as ye can.

66 So they went, and made the sepulchre sure, sealing the stone, and setting a watch.

Matthew 28

In the end of the sabbath, as it began to dawn toward the first day of the week, came Mary Magdalene and the other Mary to see the sepulchre.

2 And, behold, there was a great earthquake: **for the angel of the Lord descended from heaven, and came and rolled back the stone from the door, and sat upon it.**

3 His countenance was like lightening, and his raiment white as snow:

4 And for fear of him the keepers did shake, and became as dead men.

5 And the angel answered and said unto the women, Fear not ye: for I know that ye seek Jesus, which was crucified.

6 He is not here: for he is risen, as he said. Come, see the place where the Lord lay.

7 And go quickly, and tell his disciples that he is risen from the dead; and, behold, he goeth before you into Galilee; there shall ye see him: lo, I have told you.

8 And they departed quickly from the sepulchre with fear and great joy; and did run to bring his disciples word.

9 And as they went to tell his disciples, behold, Jesus met them, saying, All hail. And they came and held him by the feet, and worshipped him.

10 Then said Jesus unto them, Be not afraid: go tell my brethren that they go into Galilee, and there shall they see me.

11 Now when they were going, behold, some of the watch came into the city, and shewed unto the chief priests all the things that were done.

12 And when they were assembled with the elders, and had taken counsel, they gave large money unto the soldiers,

13 Saying, Say ye, His disciples came by night, and stole him away while we slept.

Night is used to refer to timing. Not generally speaking as to one day or one night, although God is not limited (Ruth 4:13 So Boaz took Ruth, and she was his wife: and when he went in unto her, the LORD gave her conception, and she bear a son.) **But night is often referred to a season of time or a process of time. A period in which a situation may appear to be dark, in that one can't see how it will all work out. A season of time is how long it last and a process of time is what has to happen during this time. One thing is sure that there is a beginning and an ending, set by God.**

Ester, was with the King for one night, a season of time, that changed the history of a nation. Est 4:14 For if thou altogether holdest thy peace at this time, then shall there enlargement and deliverance arise to the Jews from another place; but thou and thy father's house shall be destroyed: and who knoweth whether thou art come to the kingdom for such a time as this?

Ruth, was with the King for one night, a process of time, that prepared her for Boaz. Ruth 3:10-11 And he said, Blessed be thou of the LORD, my daughter: for thou hast shewed more kindness in the latter end than at the beginning, inasmuch as thou followedst not young men, whether poor or rich.

And now, my daughter, fear not; I will do to thee all that thou requirest: for all the city of my people doth know that thou art a virtuous woman.

No one knows how long a night, season or process can last. 2 Peter 3:8

But, beloved, be not ignorant of this one thing, that one day is with the Lord as a thousand years, and a thousand years as one day. **God's time is not set with our clocks.**

Peter and John

Acts 5: 17- 29;

17 Then the high priest rose up, and all they that were with him, (which is the sect of the Sadducees,) and were filled with indignation,

18 And laid their hands on the apostles, and put them in the common prison.

19 But the angel of the Lord by night opened the prison doors, and brought them forth, and said,

20 Go, stand and speak in the temple to the people all the words of this life. Testify

21 And when they heard that, they entered into the temple early in the morning, and taught. But the high priest came, and they that were with him, and called the council together, and all the senate of the children of Israel and sent to the prison to have them brought.

22 But when the officers came, and found them not in the prison, they returned, and told,

23 Saying, The prison truly found we shut with all safety, and the keepers standing without before the doors: but when we had opened, we found no man within. The enemy thought he had them bound in confinement, BUT GOD!

24 Now when the high priest and the captain of the temple and the chief priests heard these things, they doubted of them whereunto this would grow. They doubted that they would go back to what got them in trouble.

25 Then came one and told them, saying, Behold, the men whom ye put in prison are standing in the temple, and teaching the people. The very thing they were told not to do.

26 Then went the captain with the officers, and brought them without violence: for they feared the people, lest they should have been stoned.

27 And when they had brought them, they set them before the council: and the high priest asked them,

28 Saying, Did not we straitly command you that ye should not teach in this name? and, behold, ye have filled Jerusalem with your doctrine, and intend to bring this man's blood upon us.

29 Then Peter and the other apostles answered and said, We ought to obey God rather than men. Do not fear man above God! God can handle man, but man can't handle God!!

Does this story sound familiar? The Father will never asks us to do anything that Jesus has not already done.

Acts 12:1-11

1 Now about that time Herod the king stretched forth his hands to vex certain of the church.

2 And he killed James the brother of John with the sword.

3 And because he saw it pleased the Jews, he proceeded further to take Peter also. (Then were the days of unleavened bread.)

4 And when he had apprehended him, he put him in prison, and delivered him to four quaternion of soldiers to keep him; intending after Easter to bring him forth to the people.

5 Peter therefore was kept in prison: but prayer was made without ceasing of the church unto God for him. They were in houses but the people were filled with the Holy Spirit, therefore they were The church.

6 And when Herod would have brought him forth, the same night Peter was sleeping between two soldiers, bound with two chains: and the keepers before the door kept the prison.

7 And, behold, the angel of the Lord came upon him, and a light shined in the prison: and he smote Peter on the side, and raised him up, saying, Arise up quickly. And his chains fell off from his hands.

8 And the angel said unto him, Gird thyself, and bind on thy sandals. And so he did. And he saith unto him, Cast thy garment about thee, and follow me. Only by his OBEDIENCE was he made free. He had to be willing to follow the Angel's instructions.

9 And he went out, and followed him; and wist not that it was true which was done by the angel; but thought he saw a vision.

10 When they were past the first and the second ward, they came unto the iron gate that leadeth unto the city; which opened to them of his own accord: and they went out, and passed on through one street; and forthwith the angel departed from him.

11 And when Peter was come to himself, he said, Now I know of a surety, that the Lord hath sent his angel, and hath delivered me out of the hand of Herod, and from all the expectation of the people of the Jews.

Acts 12:19

And when Herod had sought for him, and found him not, he examined the keepers, and commanded that they should be put to death. And he went down from Judea to Caesarea, and there abode.

The Process of Light
Acts 12:7

1. Light shined in prison

A) Prison begins in your mind, being held captive. IICorn. 10: 4-6

4 For the weapons of our warfare are not carnal, but mighty through God to the pulling down of strong holds;)

5 Casting down every imagination, and every high thing that exalteth itself against the knowledge of God, and bringing into captivity every thought to the obedience of Christ;

6 And having in a readiness to revenge all disobedience, when your obedience is fulfilled.

B) The word of God brings light. I John 1:5

This then is the message which we have heard of him, and declare unto you, that God is light, and in him is no darkness at all.

Thy word is a lamp unto my feet and a light unto me path. Ps.119:104

C) **The word takes captive and releases angels to avenge all disobedience Ps. 103:20 – 21**

Bless the LORD, ye his angels; that excel in strength, that do his commandments, hearkening unto the voice of his word.

Bless ye the LORD, all ye his hosts; ye ministers of his, that do his pleasure.

The word raised him up, strengthened him, and set him free from the weapon of the enemy.

The Process of God's Vengeance
"with angelic assistance"
Acts 12:8

2. Put on **armour** for the journey; moving to your new address!

Gird thyself Eph. 6:14 Stand therefore, having your loins girt about with truth,(**the word of God will destroy any weapon that the enemy might come up with, before the angel has gotten you to safety**) and having on the breastplate of righteousness;

I Peter 1:13 Wherefore gird up the loins of your mind,(**the battle is in the mind**) be sober, and hope to the end for the **grace** that is to be brought unto you at the **revelation** of Jesus Christ; **II Peter 1:2** Grace and peace be multiplied unto you through the knowledge of God, and of Jesus our Lord. **Grace is only given at the level in which we know or have the revelation of Him. And the more we know or have the revelation of Him, the more peace we will have. Matt.16:18 And the gates of hell can not prevail!**

C) Bind on thy Sandals Eph. 6:15

And your feet shod with the preparation of the gospel of peace; **We must Walk It OUT! Luke 10:19** Behold, I give unto you power to tread on serpents and scorpions, and over all the power of the enemy: and nothing shall by any means hurt you.

D) Cast thy garment about thee Rev 19:8 And to her was granted that she should be arrayed in fine linen, clean and white: for the fine linen is the righteousness of saints. **This Robe of Righteousness is the Covenant of God. It is pure and holy, without spot or blemish. Isa 54:17** No weapon that is formed against thee shall prosper; and every tongue that shall rise against thee in judgment thou shalt condemn. This is the heritage of the servants of the LORD, and **their righteousness is of me**, saith the LORD.

When we do it God's way, totally trusting Him, He will bring us safely through Matt 6:33 But seek ye first the kingdom of God, and his righteousness; and all these things shall be added unto you.

E) And Follow Me," Obedience" Is. 40:3-8

3 The voice of him that crieth in the wilderness, Prepare ye the way of the LORD, make straight in the desert a highway for our God. **The word of God goes before preparing the way. Where His word is, there will He be also. Just as John the Baptist (the word) was the fore runner, the best man, whose purpose was to escort the bride to her groom. But when Jesus, the groom showed up, John had to step down, his purpose was fulfilled. The word of God must go before Him, to escort us into His presence, but when he manifest, the word steps down, fulfilling it's purpose.**

4 Every valley shall be exalted, and every mountain and hill shall be made low: and the crooked shall be made straight, and the rough places plain:

5 And the glory of the LORD shall be revealed, and all flesh shall see it together: for the mouth of the LORD hath spoken it.

6 The voice said, Cry. And he said, What shall I cry? All flesh is grass, and all the goodliness thereof is as the flower of the field:

7 The grass withereth, the flower fadeth: because the spirit of the LORD bloweth upon it: surely the people is grass.

8 The grass withereth, the flower fadeth: but the word of our God shall stand for ever. **Cry the Word of God! It will walk you through the valley of the shadow of death, to the table prepared before you in the presence of your enemies. Ps 23 The Word is our Shepard!**

Acts 12:10, When they were past the first and the second ward, they came unto the iron gate that leadeth unto the city; which opened to **them** of **his own accord**: and they went out, and passed on through one street; and forthwith the angel departed from him. **The angel stayed with Peter, as long as he responded according to his commands. Peter trusted God**

to deliver him and he had to believe that the angel, was sent by God. And whatever instructions the angel gave had to come from God. Just as the Angels hearken unto the voice of the word of God when we speak His word, we must hearken unto the voice of the words of God when the angel speaks to us. The angel stayed with Peter until he had gotten him to safety.

12:11 God flipped the script on the enemy, instead of was a table prepared before him in the presence of his enemies. Isa 55:11-13 So shall my word be that goeth forth out of my mouth: it shall not return unto me void, but it shall accomplish that which I please, and it shall prosper in the thing whereto I sent it.

12 For ye shall go out with joy, and be led forth with peace: the mountains and the hills shall break forth before you into singing, and all the trees of the field shall clap their hands.

13 Instead of the thorn shall come up the fir tree, and instead of the brier shall come up the myrtle tree: and it shall be to the LORD for a name, for an everlasting sign, (**Covenant**) that shall not be cut off. **Because is has been established in Righteousness and the word of God abideth forever Is. 40:8**

The word of God brings change. "Instead of", calling those things that be not as though they were. Instead of death there is Life, instead of fear there is Power, Love and a Sound Mind, instead of confusion there is Peace, instead of sorrow there is Joy. Flip the Script!

12:23-24

And immediately the angel of the Lord smote him, because he gave not God the glory: and he was eaten of worms, and gave up the ghost.

But the word of God grew and multiplied.

The angel of the Lord smote Peter's enemy. The weapon that was intended to stop the word, could not prosper. God will not always deliver us from righteous suffering, but through righteous suffering,

just know that God has a bigger plan in mind, a greater glory. And it's all designed to destroy our enemies, the enemies of God.

Prov 11:8 The righteous is delivered out of trouble, and the wicked cometh **in his stead. "Instead of"**

Ps 35:8

Let destruction come upon him at unawares; and let his net that he hath hid catch himself: into that very destruction let him fall.

Ps 7:15

He made a pit, and digged it, and is fallen into the ditch which he made.

Prov 26:27

Whoso diggeth a pit shall fall therein: and he that rolleth a stone, it will return upon him.

Ps 57:6

They have prepared a net for my steps; my soul is bowed down: they have digged a pit before me, into the midst whereof they are fallen themselves. Selah.

Ps 33:10

The LORD bringeth the counsel of the heathen to nought: he maketh the devices of the people of none effect. **It Won't Prosper!**

Ps 33:11

The counsel of the LORD **standeth for ever**, the thoughts of his heart to all generations. **Dominate!**

Ps 64

1 Hear my voice, O God, in my prayer: preserve my life from fear of the enemy.

2 Hide me from the secret counsel of the wicked; from the insurrection of the workers of iniquity:

3 Who whet their tongue like a sword, and bend their bows to shoot their arrows, even bitter words:

4 That they may shoot in secret at the perfect: suddenly do they shoot at him, and fear not.

5 They encourage themselves in an evil matter: they commune of laying snares privily; they say, Who shall see them?

6 They search out iniquities; they accomplish a diligent search: both the inward thought of every one of them, and the heart, is deep.

7 But God shall shoot at them with an arrow; **suddenl**y shall they be wounded.

8 So they shall make their **own** tongue to fall upon themselves: all that see them shall flee away.

9 all men shall fear, and shall declare the work of God; for they shall wisely consider of his doing.

10 The **righteous** shall be glad in the LORD, and shall trust in him; and all the upright in heart shall glory. **We end in Glory!**

II

A Living Sacrifice

1 I beseech you therefore, brethren, by the mercies of God, that ye present your bodies a living sacrifice, holy, acceptable unto God, which is your reasonable service. **Rom 12:1**

Renewing Our Heritage of Faith
God always has a man (or woman), is it you?
II Chronicles 6:14-42, 7:11-22 *Key verses 14-15

2 Chron 6:14-16

14 And said, O LORD God of Israel, there is no God like thee in the heaven, nor in the earth; which keepest covenant, and shewest mercy unto thy servants, that walk before thee with all their hearts:

15 Thou which hast kept with thy servant David my father that which thou hast promised him; and spakest with thy mouth, and hast fulfilled it with thine hand, as it is this day.

16 Now therefore, O LORD God of Israel, keep with thy servant David my father that which thou hast promised him, saying, There shall not fail thee a man in my sight to sit upon the throne of Israel; yet so that thy children take heed to their way to walk in my law, as thou hast walked before me.

Solomon knew his father was a man after God's heart and he saw how God blessed and strengthened him. So he cries out in prayer for God to bless the work of his hands and to cover his Kingdom, just as he had promised his father. II Sam 7:12-16

12 And when thy days be fulfilled, and thou shalt sleep with thy fathers, I will set up thy seed after thee, which shall proceed out of thy bowels, and I will establish his kingdom.

13 He shall build an house for my name, and I will stablish the throne of his kingdom for ever.

14 I will be his father, and he shall be my son. If he commit iniquity, I will chasten him with the rod of men, and with the stripes of the children of men:

15 But my mercy shall not depart away from him, as I took it from Saul, whom I put away before thee.

16 And thine house and thy kingdom shall be established for ever before thee: thy throne shall be established for ever. **God spoke it first!**

When God speaks it first, it then becomes activated and we then are authorized to use it for eternity. We can not just take God's word and control him. When it becomes Ramah it is in it's season and is a work while yet being spoken. God speaks his word in his time. Even though his word can not return void, it is only activated in it's season.

Renewed the Vision – kept hope alive

Every generation should build upon the foundation of the previous generation – Advancing.

Guaranteed security by adding a contingency clause, or support clause. This was to protect the inheritance of the Kingdom.

2 Chron 6:26

When the heaven is shut up, and there is no rain, because they have sinned against thee; yet if they pray toward this place, and confess thy name, and turn from their sin, when thou dost afflict them; Because of Israel's history of falling into sin (generation of iniquity). The curse was passed on to the children. If children are not serving God, there should not be a will left for them. We are only inheritors by accepting Jesus as our Savior and Lord, through a life of faith and obedience. And if we choose not to, then we are not partakers his will, so why should our children be. **We are all held accountable for our choices!** Ezekiel 18:14-24

14 Now, lo, if he beget a son, that seeth all his father's sins which he hath done, and considereth, and doeth not such like,

15 That hath not eaten upon the mountains, neither hath lifted up his eyes to the idols of the house of Israel, hath not defiled his neighbour's wife,

16 Neither hath oppressed any, hath not withholden the pledge, neither hath spoiled by violence, but hath given his bread to the hungry, and hath covered the naked with a garment,

17 That hath taken off his hand from the poor, that hath not received usury nor increase, hath executed my judgments, hath walked in my statutes; he shall not die for the iniquity of his father, he shall surely live.

18 As for his father, because he cruelly oppressed, spoiled his brother by violence, and did that which is not good among his people, lo, even he shall die in his iniquity.

19 Yet say ye, Why? doth not the son bear the iniquity of the father? When the son hath done that which is lawful and right, and hath kept all my statutes, and hath done them, he shall surely live.

20 The soul that sinneth, it shall die. The son shall not bear the iniquity of the father, neither shall the father bear the iniquity of the son: the righteousness of the righteous shall be upon him, and the wickedness of the wicked shall be upon him.

21 But if the wicked will turn from all his sins that he hath committed, and keep all my statutes, and do that which is lawful and right, he shall surely live, he shall not die.

22 All his transgressions that he hath committed, they shall not be mentioned unto him: in his righteousness that he hath done he shall live.

23 Have I any pleasure at all that the wicked should die? saith the Lord GOD: and not that he should return from his ways, and live?

24 But when the righteous turneth away from his righteousness, and committeth iniquity, and doeth according to all the abominations that the wicked man doeth, shall he live? All his righteousness that he hath done shall not be mentioned: in his trespass that he hath trespassed, and in his sin that he hath sinned, in them shall he die.

No one is exempt!

II Chronicles 6:27-30

7 Then hear thou from heaven, and forgive the sin of thy servants, and of thy people Israel, when thou hast taught them the good way, wherein they should walk; and send rain upon thy land, which thou hast given unto thy people for an inheritance.

28 If there be dearth in the land, if there be pestilence, if there be blasting, or mildew, locusts, or caterpillers; if their enemies besiege them in the cities of their land; whatsoever sore or whatsoever sickness there be:

29 Then what prayer or what supplication soever shall be made of any man, or of all thy people Israel, when every one shall know his own sore and his own grief, and shall spread forth his hands in this house:

30 Then hear thou from heaven thy dwelling place, and forgive, and render unto every man according unto all his ways, whose heart thou knowest; (for thou only knowest the hearts of the children of men:) **God knows our hearts. It's not for others to see, but in sincerity and truth.** Joel 1:3 Tell

ye your children of it, and let your children tell their children, and their children another generation.

Joel 2:12-13 Therefore also now, saith the LORD, turn ye even to me with all your heart, and with fasting, and with weeping, and with mourning:

13 And rend your heart, and not your garments, and turn unto the LORD your God: for he is gracious and merciful, slow to anger, and of great kindness, and repenteth him of the evil. **The sacrifices of God are a broken spirit: a broken and a contrite heart, O God, thou wilt not despise. Ps 51:17**

2 Chron 7:6-8:1

7 Moreover Solomon hallowed the middle of the court that was before the house of the LORD: for there he offered burnt offerings, and the fat of the peace offerings, because the brasen altar which Solomon had made was not able to receive the burnt offerings, and the meat offerings, and the fat.

Also at the same time Solomon kept the feast seven days, and all Israel with him, a very great congregation, from the entering in of Hamath unto the river of Egypt.

9 And in the eighth day they made a solemn assembly: for they kept the dedication of the altar seven days, and the feast seven days.

10 And on the three and twentieth day of the seventh month he sent the people away into their tents, glad and merry in heart for the goodness that the LORD had shewed unto David, and to Solomon, and to Israel his people.

11 Thus Solomon **finished** the house of the LORD, and the king's house: and all that came into Solomon's heart to make in the house of the LORD, and in his own house, he prosperously effected. **God's favor is always there to fulfill His purpose.**

12 And the LORD appeared to Solomon by night, and said unto him, I have heard thy prayer, and have chosen this place to myself for an house of sacrifice.

13 If I shut up heaven that there be no rain, or if I command the locusts to devour the land, or if I send pestilence among my people;

14 If my people, which are called by my name, shall humble themselves, and pray, and seek my face, and turn from their wicked ways; then will I hear from heaven, and will forgive their sin, and will heal their land.

15 Now mine eyes shall be open, and mine ears attent unto the prayer that is made in this place. **Granted request! 1) let your request be made known. 2) Be specific. 3) Believe, according to His will and your faith, God answers. There is Grace for Dream Fulfillment.**

16 For **now** have I chosen and sanctified this house, that my name may be there for: and mine eyes and mine heart shall be there perpetually. **Now, always active, present tense, His word.**

17 And as for thee, if thou wilt walk before me, as David thy father walked, and do according to all that I have commanded thee, and shalt observe my statues and my judgments; **"As for thee, if thou wilt", 1) One must be willing to follow God's plan or command. 2) That "one" will always be "Chosen" by God for the assignment, good or bad. 3) It only takes one man to establish the blessing, or the curse! 4) Leadership determines the flow of the blessing.** Gal 3:13 Christ hath redeemed us from the curse of the law, being made a curse for us: for it is written, Cursed is every one that hangeth on a tree:

18 Then will I stablish the throne of thy kingdom, according as I have covenanted with David thy father, saying, There shall not fail thee a man to be ruler in Israel.

Then, As you live according to God's will, He does. God does not make deals with us concerning His will. So stop trying to get Him to change His mind. He would have to replay His creation backwards and start all over. It ain't happening!

19 But if ye turn away, and forsake my statutes and my commandments, which I have set before you, and shall go and serve other gods, and worship them;

20 Then will I pluck them up by the roots out of my land which I have given them; and this house, which I have sanctified for my name, will I cast out of my sight, and will make it to be a proverb and a byword among all nations." **But if ye, before you, Then I will pluck them". The visionary has to stay focused, the lives of others are hanging in the balance. We lead by example. Matt 10:25** It is enough for the disciple that he be as his master, and the servant as his lord. If they have called the master of the house Beelzebub, how much more shall they call them of his household? **3) The head determines what the body will be. Leadership determines the flow of the anointing. Rom 5:12-21** Wherefore, as by one man sin entered into the world, and death by sin; and so death passed upon all men, for that all have sinned:

13(For until the law sin was in the world: but sin is not imputed when there is no law.

14 Nevertheless death reigned from Adam to Moses, even over them that had not sinned after the similitude of Adam's transgression, who is the figure of him that was to come.

15 But not as the offence, so also is the free gift. For if through the offence of one many be dead, much more the grace of God, and the gift by grace, which is by one man, Jesus Christ, hath abounded unto many.

16 And not as it was by one that sinned, so is the gift: for the judgment was by one to condemnation, but the free gift is of many offences unto justification.

17 For if by one man's offence death reigned by one; much more they which receive abundance of grace and of the gift of righteousness shall reign in life by one, Jesus Christ.)

18 Therefore as by the offence of one judgment came upon all men to condemnation; even so by the righteousness of one the free gift came upon all men unto justification of life.

19 For as by one man's disobedience many were made sinners, so by the obedience of one shall many be made righteous.

20 Moreover the law entered, that the offence might abound. But where sin abounded, grace did much more abound:

21 That as sin hath reigned unto death, even so might grace reign through righteousness unto eternal life by Jesus Christ our Lord.

II Chronicles 6:21-22 And this house, which is high, shall be an astonishment to every one that passeth by it; so that he shall say, Why hath the LORD done thus unto this land, and unto this house?

22 And it shall be answered, Because they forsook the LORD God of their fathers, which brought them forth out of the land of Egypt, and laid hold on other gods, and worshipped them, and served them: therefore hath he brought all this evil upon them.

It only takes one faithful leader to establish the blessing and one rebellious leader to mess things up.

Positioned for Purpose
Ester 2:7-9:22
The Palace was a Place of Preparation
that Positioned Ester for Purpose.

This story sounds all too, familiar. Just like Joseph, Ester too, had to endure a pit, a prison, and a palace, all places of preparation, positioning her for purpose.

"The Pit and the Prison"

Ester 2:7 And he brought up Hadassah, that is, Esther, his uncle's daughter: for she had neither father nor mother, and the maid was fair and beautiful; whom Mordecai, when her father and mother were dead, took for his own daughter. God has purpose for all that we go through in life and nothing is in vain. The people that raise us, is not coincidental or by happen stance, it's all part of God's ultimate plan. The death of her parents, being raised by her uncle and even being carried away captive was part of God's plan to position her for purpose. It was her **Destiny.** So no matter what is going on in your life, just **REST** assured that, **God is in control! Rom 8:28** And we know that all things work together for good to them that love God, to them who are the **called** according to his purpose.

" The Preparation"

Ester 2:9 And the maiden pleased him, and she obtained kindness of him; and he speedily gave her her things for purification, with such things as belonged to her, and seven maidens, which were meet to be given her, out of the king's house: and he preferred her and her maids unto the best place of the house of the women.

Ester pleased Him, she graced Him with her presence. What she possessed inside reflected in all her actions. Her talk, her walk, the way she looked, her countenance. The things she had to endure growing up without mother and father produced character. Humility, gratefulness, gentleness, goodness, meekness, love, temperance, joy, peace, faith longsuffering, endurance, determination, confidence, boldness, excellence, integrity and the list goes on. Ester was a fighter, a survivor from within that showed from without. God knows what situation to put us in to lay a good strong foundation for what He has planned, for life is the process.

God had already **chosen** from birth and **processed** Ester for her position as queen, by what she had overcome. Now it was time for her to be **positioned.** Though God ordained and purified in life's fires, Ester now had to now follow man's process of being crowned queen. She was ahead of all the other women.

he preferred her and her maids unto the best place of the house of the women. God always gives His best when rewarding for a job well done. This was only the beginning of God's favor. Ester had come through quite an ordeal, many didn't make it. But when chosen, God graces you to endure.

Ester 2:15

Now when the turn of Esther, the daughter of Abihail the uncle of Mordecai, who had taken her for his daughter, was come to go in unto the king, she required nothing but what Hegai the king's chamberlain, the keeper of the women, appointed. And Esther obtained favour in the sight of all them that looked upon her. **Ester was a ready: and require only what the King appointed for that step in man's process. Her beauty flowed from within. She was strengthened in her inner man. Rom 8:28-30** And we know that all things work together for good to them that love God, to them who are the called according to his purpose.

29 For whom he did foreknow, he also did predestinate to be conformed to the image of his Son, that he might be the firstborn among many brethren.

30 Moreover whom he did predestinate, them he also called: and whom he called, them he also justified: and whom he justified, them he also glorified. **Prov 18:16**

A man's gift maketh room for him, and bringeth him before great men.

And Esther obtained favour in the sight of all them that looked upon her. Ester had favor with God and Man.

"The Position"

Ester 2:17

And the king loved Esther above all the women, and she obtained grace and favour in his sight more than all the virgins; so that he set the royal crown upon her head, and made her queen instead of Vashti. The King – Grace and Favor, Ester was walking in the blessing all the time, but now on another level. She was pregnant with promotion. It must first be in us. **Phil 2:13** For it is God which worketh in you both to will and to do of his good pleasure. The glory, for His inheritance **Eph 1:18** The eyes of your understanding being enlightened; that ye may know what is the hope of his calling, and what the riches of the glory **of his inheritance** in the saints. **What has God invested in you that He is wanting and waiting for His return?**

"The Purpose"

Ester3:13

And the letters were sent by posts into all the king's provinces, to destroy, to kill, and to cause to perish, all Jews, both young and old, little children and women, in one day, even upon the thirteenth day of the twelfth month, which is the month Adar, and to take the spoil of them for a prey.

1) God placed Ester in a place of authority that she might save her kindred from the decree made by the enemy

2) To act as intercessor, Ester 4:14 For if thou altogether holdest thy peace at this time, then shall there enlargement and deliverance arise to the Jews from another place; but thou and thy father's house shall be destroyed: and who knoweth whether thou art come to the kingdom for such a time as this? For such a time as this; God is not a God of time but of timing.

3) To show forth the exceeding greatness of His power, Eph 1:19 And what is the exceeding greatness of his power to usward who believe, according to the working of his mighty power. God set Ester in position to show himself off. Ester **5:2** And it was so, when the king saw Esther the queen standing in the court, that she obtained favour in his sight: and the king held out to Esther the golden sceptre that was in his hand. So Esther drew near, and touched the top of the sceptre.

"God's Plan In Motion"

Ester fed the spirit of PRIDE that controlled (the enemy) Haman. Ester 5: 4-9a

And Esther answered, If it seem good unto the king, let the king and Haman come this day unto the banquet that I have prepared for him.

5 Then the king said, Cause Haman to make haste, that he may do as Esther hath said. So the king and Haman came to the banquet that Esther had prepared.

6 And the king said unto Esther at the banquet of wine, What is thy petition? and it shall be granted thee: and what is thy request? even to the half of the kingdom it shall be performed.

7 Then answered Esther, and said, My petition and my request is;

8 If I have found favour in the sight of the king, and if it please the king to grant my petition, and to perform my request, let the king and Haman come to the banquet that I shall prepare for them, and I will do tomorrow as the king hath said.

9 Then went Haman forth that day joyful and with a glad heart: but when Haman saw Mordecai in the king's gate, that he stood not up, nor moved for him, he was full of indignation against Mordecai.

The enemy takes the bait! Est 5:11-12

And Haman told them of the glory of his riches, and the multitude of his children, and all the things wherein the king had promoted him, and how he had advanced him above the princes and servants of the king.

12 Haman said moreover, Yea, Esther the queen did let no man come in with the king unto the banquet that she had prepared but myself; and to morrow am I invited unto her also with the king.

5) God puts the plan in the enemies mouth and then uses it against him, that it blesses you. Ester 5:14 Then said Zeresh his wife and all his friends unto him, Let a gallows be made of fifty cubits high, and tomorrow speak thou unto the king that Mordecai may be hanged thereon: then go thou in merrily with the king unto the banquet. And the thing pleased Haman; and he caused the gallows to be made.

6) God will fight for you! He knows how to set you up. Ester 6:1-10

1 On that night could not the king sleep, and he commanded to bring the book of records of the chronicles; and they were read before the king.

2 And it was found written, that Mordecai had told of Bigthana and Teresh, two of the king's chamberlains, the keepers of the door, who sought to lay hand on the king Ahasuerus.

3 And the king said, What honour and dignity hath been done to Mordecai for this? Then said the king's servants that ministered unto him, There is nothing done for him.

4 And the king said, Who is in the court? Now Haman was come into the outward court of the king's house, to speak unto the king to hang Mordecai on the gallows that he had prepared for him.

5 And the king's servants said unto him, Behold, Haman standeth in the court. And the king said, Let him come in.

6 So Haman came in. And the king said unto him, What shall be done unto the man whom the king delighteth to honour? Now Haman thought in his heart, To whom would the king delight to do honour more than to myself?

7 And Haman answered the king, For the man whom the king delighteth to honour,

8 Let the royal apparel be brought which the king useth to wear, and the horse that the king rideth upon, and the crown royal which is set upon his head:

9 And let this apparel and horse be delivered to the hand of one of the king's most noble princes, that they may array the man withal whom the king delighteth to honour, and bring him on horseback through the street of the city, and proclaim before him, Thus shall it be done to the man whom the king delighteth to honour.

10 Then the king said to Haman, Make haste, and take the apparel and the horse, as thou hast said, and do even so to Mordecai the Jew, that sitteth at the king's gate: let nothing fail of all that thou has spoken. Divine intervention is always a step ahead of the enemy. God is faithful to remember your acts of love towards His name. Heb 6:10 For God is not

unjust to forget your work and labor of love which you have shown toward His name, in that you have ministered to the saints, and do minister.

7) God traps and exposes the enemy. Ester 7:1-6

So the king and Haman came to banquet with Esther the queen.

2 And the king said again unto Esther on the second day at the banquet of wine, What is thy petition, queen Esther? and it shall be granted thee: and what is thy request? and it shall be performed, even to the half of the kingdom.

3 Then Esther the queen answered and said, If I have found favour in thy sight, O king, and if it please the king, let my life be given me at my petition, and my people at my request:

4 For we are sold, I and my people, to be destroyed, to be slain, and to perish. But if we had been sold for bondmen and bondwomen, I had held my tongue, although the enemy could not countervail the king's damage.

5 Then the king Ahasuerus answered and said unto Esther the queen, Who is he, and where is he, that durst presume in his heart to do so?

6 And Esther said, The adversary and enemy is this wicked Haman. Then Haman was afraid before the king and the queen.

8) Entangles enemy in his own snare. Ester 7:8-10

Then the king returned out of the palace garden into the place of the banquet of wine; and Haman was fallen upon the bed whereon Esther was. Then said the king, Will he force the queen also before me in the house? As the word went out of the king's mouth, they covered Haman's face.

9 And Harbonah, one of the chamberlains, said before the king, Behold also, the gallows fifty cubits high, which Haman had made for Mordecai, who had spoken good for the king, standeth in the house of Haman. Then the king said, Hang him thereon.

10 So they hanged Haman on the gallows that he had prepared for Mordecai. Then was the king's wrath pacified. Pacified not satisfied, this was only the beginning.

Est 8:1-5

On that day did the king Ahasuerus give the house of Haman the Jews' enemy unto Esther the queen. And Mordecai came before the king; for Esther had told what he was unto her.

2 And the king took off his ring, which he had taken from Haman, and gave it unto Mordecai. And Esther set Mordecai over the house of Haman.

3 And Esther spake yet again before the king, and fell down at his feet, and besought him with tears to put away the mischief of Haman the Agagite, and his device that he had devised against the Jews.

4 Then the king held out the golden sceptre toward Esther. So Esther arose, and stood before the king,

5 And said, If it please the king, and if I have found favour in his sight, and the thing seem right before the king, and I be pleasing in his eyes, let it be written to reverse the letters devised by Haman the son of Hammedatha the Agagite, which he wrote to destroy the Jews which are in all the king's provinces:

Ester 9:25

But when Esther came before the king, he commanded by letters that his wicked device, which he devised against the Jews, should return upon his own head, and that he and his sons should be hanged on the gallows.

10) Granted authority to use King's name. Ester 8:8

Write ye also for the Jews, as it liketh you, in the king's name, and seal it with the king's ring: for the writing which is written in the king's name, and sealed with the king's ring, may no man reverse. Just like David, Ester had conquered her Goliath, and received great riches.

11) There are rewards for not compromising. The enemies spoils. Ester 8:2

And the king took off his ring, which he had taken from Haman, and gave it unto Mordecai. And Esther set Mordecai over the house of Haman.

12) God causes the enemies plan to work in your favor. Isa 54:14-17

14 In righteousness shalt thou be established: thou shalt be far from oppression; for thou shalt not fear: and from terror; for it shall not come near thee.

15 Behold, they shall surely gather together, but not by me: whosoever shall gather together against thee shall fall for thy sake.

16 Behold, I have created the smith that bloweth the coals in the fire, and that bringeth forth an instrument for his work; and I have created the waster to destroy.

17 No weapon that is formed against thee shall prosper; and every tongue that shall rise against thee in judgment thou shalt condemn. This is the heritage of the servants of the LORD, and their righteousness is of me, saith the LORD. **The enemies attack is his assignment, to set you up for the blessing. God is in control.**

A) Who God bless, no man can curse. Num 23:20

Behold, I have received commandment to bless: and he hath blessed; and I cannot reverse it.

B) He that diggeth a pit, himself shall fall therein. **Prov 26:27**

Whoso diggeth a pit shall fall therein: and he that rolleth a stone, it will return upon him.

Eccl 10:8

8 He that diggeth a pit shall fall into it; and whoso breaketh an hedge, a serpent shall bite him.

C) every snare that is lain for thy feet, thy enemy shall be entangled in his own snare. Ps 35:8

8 Let destruction come upon him at unawares; and let his net that he hath hid catch himself: into that very destruction let him fall.

D) Every arrow shot shall return back into his own bossom. Ps 64:3-8

3 Who whet their tongue like a sword, and bend their bows to shoot their arrows, even bitter words:

4 That they may shoot in secret at the perfect: suddenly do they shoot at him, and fear not.

5 They encourage themselves in an evil matter: they commune of laying snares privily; they say, Who shall see them?

6 They search out iniquities; they accomplish a diligent search: both the inward thought of every one of them, and the heart, is deep.

7 **But God shall shoot at them with an arrow; suddenly shall they be wounded**.

8 So they shall make their own tongue to fall upon themselves: all that see them shall flee away. **The words of their own mouths shall pierce their soul!**

The Word of God Can Not Return Void!!

The Great Debater
Matt. 4:1-11

This revelation came after being inspired by the movie, The Great Debaters"; how words changed the lives of young college students. One's that were statistically said to be the underdogs or least likely. Those despised of men and rejected, but esteemed precious in the eyes of him who mentored them. Is not this a shadow of Christ, God the Father and His children? **1 Peter**

2:4 To whom coming, as unto a living stone, disallowed indeed of men, but chosen of God, and precious.

1 Cor 1:27-29

7 But God hath chosen the foolish things of the world to confound the wise; and God hath chosen the weak things of the world to confound the things, which are mighty;

28 And base things of the world, and things which are despised, hath God chosen, yea, and things which are not, to bring to nought things that are:

29 That no flesh should glory in his presence.

The Bible tells us that, **John 1:1-3** the beginning was the Word, and the Word was with God, and the Word was God.

2 The same was in the beginning with God.

3 **All** things were made by him; and without him was not any thing made that was made. So all things were made by or with the word. The Bible also tells me that, **Gen 1:1-3** In the beginning God created the heaven and the earth.

2 And the earth was without form, and void; and darkness was upon the face of the deep. And the Spirit of God **moved** upon the face of the waters.

3 And God **said**, Let there be light: and there was light. And God said through out all His creation. So God used words to create. How powerful! The Spirit of God moves and speaks; speaks and moves. But one more important thing that the Bible tells me is that, **Gen 1:27** God created man in **his own image**, in the image of God created he him; male and female created he them. Oh, my God! So you mean we are speaking spirits on the move also! No wonder God tells us that, **Prov 18:7** A fool's mouth is his destruction, and his lips are the snare of his soul.

Prov 18:21 Death and life are in the power of the tongue: and they that love it shall eat the **fruit thereof.**

Rom 4:17 As it is written, I have made thee a father of many nations,) before him whom he believed, even God, who quickeneth the dead, and calleth those things which be not as though they were.

The word of God creates, it changes Isa 55:11-13

So shall my word be that goeth forth out of my mouth: it shall not return unto me void, but it shall accomplish that which I please, and it shall prosper in the thing whereto I sent it.

12 For ye shall go out with joy, and be led forth with peace: the mountains and the hills shall break forth before you into singing, and all the trees of the field shall clap their hands.

13 **Instead of** the thorn shall come up the fir tree, and instead of the brier shall come up the myrtle tree: and it shall be to the LORD for a name, for an everlasting sign that shall not be cut off.

Matt 12:37

37 For by thy words thou shalt be **justified**, and by thy words thou shalt be condemned. Established or destroyed, you choose!

Matt 12:36

36 But I say unto you, That every idle word that men shall speak, they shall give account thereof in the day of judgment.

Matt 12:35

35 A good man out of the good treasure of the heart bringeth forth good things: and an evil man out of the evil treasure bringeth forth evil things. What are your bringing forth that's hidden in your heart?

Matt 12:34

34 O generation of vipers, how can ye, being evil, speak good things? for out of the abundance of the heart the mouth speaketh. So the only way

that I can produce good or God, It must be hidden in my heart. **1 Peter 3:15** But **sanctify** the Lord God in your hearts: and be ready always to give an answer to every man that asketh you a reason of the hope that is in you with meekness and fear:

John 12:48

He that rejecteth me, and receiveth not my words, hath one that judgeth him: the word that I have spoken, the same shall **judge** him in the last day.

Heb 12:23

Tthe general assembly and church of the firstborn, which are written in heaven, and to God the **Judge** of all, and to the spirits of just men made perfect, **Rev 19:11-16**

11 And I saw heaven opened, and behold a white horse; and he that sat upon him was called Faithful and True, and in righteousness he doth **judge** and **make war**.

12 His eyes were as a flame of fire, and on his head were many crowns; and he had a name written, that no man knew, but he himself.

13 And he was clothed with a vesture dipped in blood: and his name is called **The Word of God.**

14 And the armies which were in heaven **followe**d him upon white horses, clothed in fine linen, white and clean.

15 **And out of his mouth goeth a sharp sword**, that with it he should smite the nations: and he shall rule them with a rod of iron: and he treadeth the winepress of the fierceness and wrath of Almighty God.

16 And he hath on his vesture and on his thigh a name written, **KING OF KINGS, AND LORD OF LORDS.**

So in reality it is A Battle Of Words, The Facts-vs-The Truth!

And when it all boils down the word of God, God himself, decides the out come, and who is victorious. And if I speak the truth, that changes and creates, then the words of him who opposes me, are merely the facts, that really don't even matter; For they are the present state of my situation and can never change the truth. 2 Cor 4:17-18 For our light affliction, which is but for a moment, worketh for us a far more exceeding and eternal weight of glory; The truth of God's word.

18 While we look **not** at the things which are seen, but at the things which are not seen: for the things which are seen are temporal; **but the things which are not seen are eternal.**

Although my opponent's words are not in comparison to the truth I speak, I must be aware of his strategy or strategies. His desire is to make me question the truth I speak, to rob me of my confidence. For it is in **confidence** that I am able to project the truth with power and authority. His main weapons are doubt and fear. If he knows that I am a believer, then he must get me to doubt some parts of what I believe then cause me to fear stepping out and trusting God. **I can't destroy a lie unless I know the truth.** If it's not the truth, the whole truth and nothing but the truth, then it has no power.

James 1:7-8 For let not that man think that he shall receive any thing of the Lord. 8 A double minded man is unstable in all his ways.

Things to Know:

1) I must be confident when speaking giving my words power. Eph 3:12 In whom we have boldness and access with confidence by the faith of him.

2) My opponent takes the words I speak and tries to use them against me, twisting the truth. Jude 4 For there are certain men crept in unawares, who were before of old ordained to this condemnation, ungodly men, turning the grace of our God into lasciviousness, and denying the only Lord God, and our Lord Jesus Christ. **Jude 8** Likewise also these filthy dreamers defile the flesh, despise dominion, and speak evil of dignities.

Jude 10 But these speak evil of those things which they know not: but what they know **naturally,** as brute beasts, in those things they corrupt themselves.

3) I must study to show myself approved. 2 Tim 2:15

Study to shew thyself approved unto God, a workman that needeth not to be ashamed, rightly dividing the word of truth.

4) My words must come from a reliable creditable source. Num 23:19

God is not a man, that he should lie; neither the son of man, that he should repent: hath he said, and shall he not do it? or hath he spoken, and shall he not make it good?

Isa 55:11

So shall my word be that goeth forth out of my mouth: it shall not return unto me void, but it shall accomplish that which I please, and it shall prosper in the thing whereto I sent it.

5) I must remain focused at all times and learn to deal with distractions.

Ps 25:15 Mine eyes are ever toward the LORD; for he shall pluck my feet out of the net.

James 1:6 But let him ask in faith, nothing wavering. For he that wavereth is like a wave of the sea driven with the wind and tossed.

A Time of Testing:

Obedience always wins. It's the evidence of what you believe to be true.

You must be ready. – To stand firm you must have evidence to support your reason for obeying. You must be prepared.

You must be alert. – Stay focused, cast down every imagination and every high thing that exalts itself against, above the knowledge of God. **2 Cor 10:5-6** casting down imaginations, and every high thing that exalteth itself against the knowledge of God, and **bringing into captivity** every thought to the obedience of Christ; And having in a readiness to revenge all disobedience, **when your obedience is fulfilled.** If you don't put it in bondage, capture it, then it will capture you and put you in bondage.

Lost Battle: Genesis 3:1-6 Adam, Eve vs the serpent

Gen 3:1-5 Now the serpent was more subtil than any beast of the field which the LORD God had made. And he said unto the woman, Yea, hath God said, Ye shall not eat of every tree of the garden? And the woman said unto the serpent, We may eat of the fruit of the trees of the garden:

3 But of the fruit of the tree which is in the midst of the garden, God hath said, Ye shall not eat of it, neither shall ye touch it, lest ye die.

4 And the serpent said unto the woman, Ye shall not surely die: The beginning of defeat is when the enemy can cause you to second guess did God really mean what He said and how He said it? Seed of doubt!

5 For God doth know that in the day ye eat thereof, then your eyes shall be opened, and ye shall be as gods, knowing good and evil. The serpent drawed the woman into conversation, (debate) and twisted the truth (using her words against her). **We must always be in control. Never allow the enemy to draw you into conversation and/or debate. Resolve it then** (with "It is written"). **Take captive every thought that is contrary to what you believe or what you know that God has spoken to you.** (When you don' t take the thought captive, the thought takes you captive!) **When God first speaks to you, you must resolve it then (Rom 4:21** And being fully persuaded that, what he had promised, he was able also to perform). **You can not leave any room for the enemy to question what you believe. It is there where he plants to seed of doubt, to harvest fear; which is what he needs to bring his will to pass (Job 3:25** For the thing which I greatly feared is come upon me, and that which I was afraid of is come unto me).

Remember, fear to him, is like faith to God. If he can cause you to fear, (his will) he will cause you to move from your position, to a position

that he can devour you. When you move, you leave your position of safety, and now you are an open target and become prey to your enemy. Therefore allowing him to devour you. Gen 3:23-24 So the LORD God banished him from the Garden of Eden to work the ground from which he had been taken. 24 After he drove the man out, he placed on the east side of the Garden of Eden cherubim and a flaming sword flashing back and forth to guard the way to the tree of life. **As long as you are hidden in the word, he can not get to you, so he has to draw you out. Prov 18:10** The name of the LORD is a strong tower: the righteous runneth into it, and is safe.

Ps 91:1-11

He that dwelleth in the secret place of the most High shall abide (**stay, remain**) under the shadow of the Almighty.

2 I will say of the LORD, He is my refuge and my fortress: my God; in him will I trust.

3 Surely he shall deliver thee from the snare of the fowler, and from the noisome pestilence.

4 He shall **cover thee** with his feathers, and **under** his wings shalt thou trust: his truth (**word**) shall be thy shield and buckler.

5 Thou shalt not be afraid for the terror by night; nor for the arrow that flieth by day;

6 Nor for the pestilence that walketh in darkness; nor for the destruction that wasteth at noonday.

7 A thousand shall fall at thy side, and ten thousand at thy right hand; **but it shall not come nigh thee.**

8 Only with thine eyes shalt thou behold and see the reward of the wicked.

9 Because thou hast made the LORD, which is my refuge, even the most High, thy habitation;

10 There shall no evil befall thee, neither shall any plague come nigh thy dwelling.

11 For he shall give his angels charge over thee, to keep thee in all thy ways.

The battle is to prove that you are who you really say you are and that you **know** in whom you believe. How confident are you? Do you really understand what you are saying to be true? Your level of obedience is based on your level of true understanding, Revelation. **Who do you say that He is? You must know Him.**

Battle Won: Matt. 4:1-11 Jesus vs Satan

Matt 4:1-11

4:1 Then was Jesus led up of the Spirit into the wilderness to be tempted of the devil. The spirit led him to the place of preparation. God always knows best, let Him lead.

2 And when he had fasted forty days and forty nights, he was afterward an hungred.

3 And when the tempter came to him, he said, If thou be the Son of God, command that these stones be made bread. The enemy will always target what he studies to be your weakness. Then counter punching with a hidden accusation questioning your identity. But when you know who you are, there's no need to defend yourself.

4 But he answered and said, It is written, Man shall not live by bread alone, but by every word that proceedeth out of the mouth of God. Jesus lets him know that even though he hasn't eaten physical food, he had been sustained by an even greater source, spiritual food. The enemy tried to bring Jesus's attention to His flesh where he suspected him to be vulnerable.

5 Then the devil taketh him up into the holy city, and setteth him on a pinnacle of the temple,

6 And saith unto him, If thou be the Son of God, cast thyself down: for it is written, He shall give his angels charge concerning thee: and in their hands they shall bear thee up, lest at any time thou dash thy foot against a stone. Again he questions the knowledge of His identity, hoping to draw Him into pride. But Jesus knew he had nothing to lose and nothing to prove. When the enemy can't attack your weakness, he attacks your strength, hoping to draw you into pride.

7 Jesus said unto him, It is written again, Thou shalt not tempt the Lord thy God.

8 Again, the devil taketh him up into an exceeding high mountain, and sheweth him all the kingdoms of the world, and the glory of them;

9 And saith unto him, All these things will I give thee, if thou wilt fall down and worship me.

10 Then saith Jesus unto him, Get thee hence, Satan: for it is written, Thou shalt worship the Lord thy God, and him only shalt thou serve. Jesus was able to resist the temptations of Satan because he not only knew the will of the father (the word) but He was the will of the Father, the word. John 1:14 And the Word was made flesh, and dwelt among us, (and we beheld his glory, the glory as of the only begotten of the Father,) full of grace and truth. Therefore, Satan found nothing in Him. John 14:**30** Hereafter I will not talk much with you: for the prince of this world cometh, and hath nothing in me. Jesus was focused on His purpose and fought the distractions by **resting** in what He knew to be true.

11 Then the devil leaveth him, and, behold, angels came and ministered unto him.

We must learn to Rest in what God has already done, before the foundations of the world. Heb **4:3** For we which have believed do enter into **rest**, as he said, As I have sworn in my wrath, if they shall enter into my rest: **although the works were finished from the foundation of the world.**

Romans 14:1-23 God is the Judge and Jury!

1 Him that is weak in the faith receive ye, but not to doubtful disputations.

Don't debate, just walk it out! Beware of who you share your faith with. If the enemy can draw you into debate, then you are distracted. Speak the word only and REST!

4 Who art thou that judgest another man's servant? to his own master he standeth or falleth. Yea, he shall be holden up: for God is able to make him stand.

5 One man esteemeth one day above another: another esteemeth every day alike. Let every man be fully persuaded in his **own** mind. **Matt 9:29** Then touched he **their eyes**, saying, According to your faith be it unto you. No one has to believe it but you. You are the visionary.

11 For it is written, As I live, saith the Lord, every knee shall bow to me, and every tongue shall confess to God.

12 So then every one of us shall give account of himself to God.

13 Let us not therefore judge one another any more: but judge this rather, that no man put a stumblingblock or an occasion to fall in his brother's way. Don't be a stumbling block.

14 **I know**, and am persuaded by the Lord Jesus, that there is nothing unclean of itself: but to him that esteemeth any thing to be unclean, to him it is unclean. It's all about what's in your knowing.

17 For the kingdom of God is not meat and drink; but righteousness, and peace, and joy in the Holy Ghost.

18 For he that in these things serveth Christ is acceptable to God, and approved of men.

23 And he that doubteth is damned if he eat, because he eateth not of faith: for **whatsoever is not of faith is sin. In all things!**

The Goodness of the King
You can't tell it, let me tell it!
II Chronicles 9: 1-6

1 And when the queen of Sheba heard of the fame of Solomon, she came to prove Solomon with hard questions at Jerusalem, with a very great company, and camels that bare spices, and gold in abundance, and precious stones: and when she was come to Solomon, she communed with him of all that was in her heart.

2 And Solomon told her all her questions: and there was nothing hid from Solomon which he told her not.

3 And when the queen of Sheba had seen the wisdom of Solomon, and the house that he had built,

4 And the meat of his table, and the sitting of his servants, and the attendance of his ministers, and their apparel; his cupbearers also, and their apparel; and his ascent by which he went up into the house of the LORD; there was no more spirit in her.

5 And she said to the king, It was a true report which I heard in mine own land of thine acts, and of thy wisdom:

6 Howbeit I believed not their words, until I came, and mine eyes had seen it: and, behold, the one half of the greatness of thy wisdom was not told me: for thou exceedest the fame that I heard.

Solomon was a King of great wealth and wisdom. Queen Sheba had heard of his fame, but all that she had heard was just to stir up her appetite to know more. Actions speak louder than words. And if our lifestyles are not making others thirsty to know the God we proclaim, then we're not telling it right. **Matt 5:13** Ye are the salt of the earth: but if the salt have lost his savour, wherewith shall it be salted? it is thenceforth good for nothing, but to be cast out, and to be trodden under foot of men. To see and hear the testimony of others should create a hunger and thirst that encourages us to do even greater works. This is why we can't just accept who others say that Jesus is, we must know him for ourselves.

Matt 16:13-19 When Jesus came into the coasts of Caesarea Philippi, he asked his disciples, saying, Whom do **men** say that I the Son of man am?

14 And they said, Some say that thou art John the Baptist: some, Elias; and others, Jeremias, or one of the prophets.

15 He saith unto them, But whom say **ye** that I am? You must know him for yourself.

16 And Simon Peter answered and said, Thou art the Christ, the Son of the living God.

17 And Jesus answered and said unto him, Blessed art thou, Simon Barjona: for flesh and blood hath not revealed it unto thee, but my Father which is in heaven.

Peter had the revelation, he KNEW him!

18 And I say **also** unto thee, That thou art Peter, and upon this rock I will build my church; and the gates of hell shall not prevail against it.

19 And I will give unto thee the **keys** of the kingdom of heaven: and whatsoever thou shalt bind on earth shall be bound in heaven: and whatsoever thou shalt loose on earth shall be loosed in heaven. Without revelation, we have no access. Keys only come by way of revelation

When the woman at the well went back to the city and told of her encounter with Jesus and how he had told her all about herself, the Bible says she told **the men. That 's another revelation.**

John 4:28-42

28 The woman then left her waterpot, and went her way into the city, and saith to the men,

29 Come, see a man, which told me all things that ever I did: is not this the Christ?

30 Then they went out of the city, and came unto him. We must be willing to come out of our comfort zone to see Jesus.

31 In the mean while his disciples prayed him, saying, Master, eat.

32 But he said unto them, I have meat to eat that ye know not of.

33 Therefore said the disciples one to another, Hath any man brought him ought to eat?

34 Jesus saith unto them, My meat is to do the will of him that sent me, and to finish his work.

35 Say not ye, There are yet four months, and then cometh harvest? behold, I say unto you, Lift up your eyes, and look on the fields; for they are white already to harvest.

36 And he that reapeth receiveth wages, and gathereth fruit unto life eternal: that both he that soweth and he that reapeth may rejoice together.

37 And herein is that saying true, One soweth, and another reapeth.

38 I sent you to reap that whereon ye bestowed no labour: other men laboured, and ye are entered into their labours.

39 And **man**y of the Samaritans of that city **believed** on him for the saying of the woman, which testified, He told me all that ever I did. This was only an appetizer, to stir up their hunger and thirst.

40 So when the Samaritans were come unto (humbly) him, they besought him that he would tarry (stay) with them: and he abode there two days. **Matt 5:6 Blessed are they which do hunger and thirst after righteousness: for they shall be filled.**

41 And **many more believed** because of his **own** word; Jesus speaks to each one of us individually, where we are, meeting every need. You can't just take me at my word; you have got to get your own word. Just like He told me about me, He will tell you about you.

42 And said **unto** (they even had to humble themselves before her) the woman, When men perceive you to be nobody, God will make them respect you, when you know Him. **Now** we believe, not because of thy saying: for we have heard him ourselves, and **know** that this is indeed the Christ, the Saviour of the world. We can not just know of Him or about Him, but we have got to get in Him and allow Him to get in us. To know is to be intimate, to become one with. **John 15:5** I am the vine, ye are the branches: He that abideth in me, and I in him, the same bringeth forth much fruit: for without me ye can do nothing. **John 15:7** If ye abide in me, and my words abide in you, ye shall ask what ye will, and it shall be done unto you. Because we become one with "I Am".

II Chronicles 9:5 And she said to the king, It was a true report which I **heard** in mine own land of thine acts, and of thy wisdom:

6 Howbeit I believed not their words, until **I came**, and **mine eyes** had seen it: and, behold, the one **half** of the greatness of thy wisdom was not told me: for thou exceedest the fame that I heard. Sheba said," yes it was true what I heard, but I didn't believe it until I came to see for myself. And behold, look a here, let me tell you, the half had not been told, for now I know that there is so much more". You must taste and see for yourself. **Ps 34:8** O taste and see that the LORD is good: blessed is the man that trusteth in him. God creates a hunger with just a taste, that he can eventually open the eyes of your understanding, by revelation.

When we stop at who they say Jesus is, we don't even have half the story. Others can only tell you who he is to them, but they may be only meeting Him half way.

Matt 20:16 So the last shall be first, and the first last: for many be called, but few chosen. And when you are Chosen, you can't just go half of the way.

John 15:14-16 Ye are my friends, if ye do whatsoever I command you.

15 Henceforth I call you not servants; for the servant knoweth not what his lord doeth **(laborers not board members)** but I have called you friends; for all things that I have heard of my Father I have made known unto you.

16 Ye have not chosen me, but I have chosen you, and ordained you, that ye should go and bring forth fruit, and that your fruit should remain: that whatsoever ye shall ask of the Father in my name, he may give it you.

God has so much more. Queen Sheba came thirsty to know for herself, and because she was willing to come and see, she left with so much more than she expected. If she had just taken the word of others, she would not have had half of what the King had for her. Queen Sheba might not have known it but she was already chosen to go before the King. Her steps were ordered. The King had need of her gift. It was a rare gift, one that had never before been giving. An uncommon seed! **2 Chron 9:9** And she gave the king an hundred and twenty talents of gold, and of spices great abundance, and precious stones: neither was there any such spice as the queen of Sheba gave king Solomon. Never go before the King without a gift. When chosen, God requires of you more than others; your gift is not just a gift, but a sacrifice. But it's all a part of God's plan for the harvest needed to do what is required. No matter what God is requiring of you to bring, I want you to know, you **ain't gonna lose nothing!** God is trying to get something to you. You will leave with what you brought and some. II Chronicles 9:12 12 And king Solomon gave to the queen of Sheba **all** her desire, whatsoever she asked, beside that which she had brought unto the king. So she turned, and went away to her own land, she and her servants. God will honor and cover your sacrifice with his covenant, just like he did for Abram. **Gen 15:9-12** And he said unto him, Take me an heifer of three years old, and a she goat of three years old, and a ram of three years old, and a turtledove, and a young pigeon.

10 And he took unto him all these, and divided them in the midst, and laid each piece one against another: but the birds divided he not.

11 And when the fowls came down upon the carcases, Abram drove them away.

12 And when the sun was going down, a **deep sleep** fell upon Abram; and, lo, an horror of great darkness fell upon him. No need for you to stay up watching over your sacrifice, God neither slumber nor sleeps. Ps 121:4 Behold, he that keepeth Israel shall neither slumber nor sleep.

Gen 15:17-18

And it came to pass, that, when the sun went down, and it was dark, behold a smoking furnace, and a burning lamp that passed between those pieces.

18 In the same day the LORD made a **covenant** with Abram, saying, Unto thy seed have I given this land, from the river of Egypt unto the great river, the river Euphrates. **Gal 3:29** And if ye be Christ's, then are ye Abraham's seed, and heirs according to the promise.

This was all a set up to advance the Kingdom. All we have is a righteous seed. You can never go into another king's territory and out give him. And no matter how much you give, **you can't beat God giving!**

2 Chron 9:13

Now the weight of gold that came to Solomon in one year was six hundred and threescore and six talents of gold. The gold represents God's glory. It blesses the King to bless you when you are a giver, a worshipper, he knows that it's being invested into the Kingdom. You ought to let God bless himself. All He needs is our obedience, and he will do the rest. **Eph 1:18-19** The eyes of your understanding being enlightened; that ye may know what is the hope of his calling, and what the riches of the glory of **his** inheritance in the saints, God wants a return on His investment.

19 And what is the exceeding greatness of his power to usward who believe, according to the working of his mighty power, He wants to show himself strong in our lives and bring glory to His name. He needs us to believe that He is who He says that he is.

III

The Process

That the trial of your faith, being much more precious than of gold that perisheth, though it be tried with fire, might be found unto praise and honour and glory at the appearing of Jesus Christ: 1 Peter 1:7

Purposed for the Process, Processed for Purpose

Luke 22:31-34 key verse*31 Matt. 16:21-26

Say what you mean and mean what you say!

Luke 22:31-34

31 And the Lord said, Simon, Simon, behold, Satan hath desired to have you, that he may sift you as wheat:

Satan would use the very words that Peter spoke to challenge him, which would bring about this sifting.

32 But I have prayed for thee, that thy faith, fail not: and when thou art converted, strengthen thy brethren. Jesus knew the call that was on Peter's life which was of great influence.

33 And he said unto him, Lord, I am ready to go with thee, both into prison, and to death.

34 And he said, I tell thee, Peter, the cock shall not crow this day, before that thou shalt thrice deny that thou knowest me. But Jesus also knew Peter's weakness which was a great hinderance.

Matthew 16:21-26 **Main Agenda**

21 From that time forth began Jesus to shew unto his disciples, how that he must go unto Jerusalem, and suffer many things of the elders and chief priests and scribes, and be killed, and be raised again the third day.

22 Then Peter took him, and began to rebuke him, saying, Be it far from thee, Lord: this shall not be unto thee.

23 But he turned, and said unto Peter, Get thee behind me, Satan: thou art an offence unto me: for thou savourest not the things that be of God, but those that be of men. Peter didn't want Jesus to go through and suffer because he knew that it would mean that he would have to suffer. And though he spoke well with his mouth, his heart was far from it. Peter wanted it to appear that he was concerned and yet thoughtful concerning Jesus. He didn't realize that Satan had a holt on him and his agenda was to use Peter's weakness to destroy his willingness, hoping to influence Jesus not to go. But Jesus saw the root of Peter's dilemma and rebuked it.

24 Then said Jesus unto his disciples, If any man will come after me, let him deny himself, and take up his cross, and follow me.

25 For whosoever will save his life shall lose it: and whosoever will lose his life for my sake shall find it.

26 For what is a man profited, if he shall gain the whole world, and lose his own soul? or what shall a man give in exchange for his soul?

Satan knew that there was no way that he could stop Jesus, so his alternate agenda was to stop Peter from becoming a true disciple. Satan knows the danger in multiplication.

Matt 16:13-19

13 When Jesus came into the coasts of Caesarea Philippi, he asked his disciples, saying, Whom do men say that I the Son of man am?

14 And they said, Some say that thou art John the Baptist: some, Elias; and others, Jeremias, or one of the prophets.

15 He saith unto them, But whom say **ye** that I am?

16 And Simon Peter answered and said, Thou art the Christ, the Son of the living God.

17 And Jesus answered and said unto him, Blessed art thou, Simon Barjona: for flesh and blood hath not revealed it unto thee, but my Father which is in heaven.

18 And I say also unto thee, That thou art Peter, and upon this rock I will build my church; and the gates of hell shall not prevail against it.

19 And I will give unto thee the keys of the kingdom of heaven: and whatsoever thou shalt bind on earth shall be bound in heaven: and whatsoever thou shalt loose on earth shall be loosed in heaven.

Peter has gotten the Revelation of who Jesus is. Jesus wanted him to know that along with him getting the revelation from the Father, he also received power and authority, which were keys, granting access into the Kingdom. But the revelation Peter didn't get was who he was and the ability he had to tap into that power and authority he had been given. We cannot be successful in knowing who Jesus is and deny his power and ability to rule in our lives. Many of us don't know that he has given us this same power and authority. And yet are waiting for him to do it. Well guess what? He's waiting for you to do it!

So Jesus wants Peter to know that Satan has desired, he has asked for permission to try you, and I have granted it, but I have already prayed that your faith would not fail you. **Isa 54:16-17** Behold, I have created the smith that bloweth the coals in the fire, and that bringeth forth an instrument for his work; and I have created the waster to destroy. What God allows Satan to do, is for the furtherance of His work. He, (God) allows him to use or create his weapon of choice, in a controlled environment, but promises that,

17 **No weapon that is formed against thee shall prosper**; and every tongue that shall rise against thee in judgment thou shalt condemn. This is the heritage of the servants of the LORD, and their righteousness is of me, saith the LORD.

Be careful what you say. Say what you mean and mean what you say. God will allow Satan to call you on the carpet, that he may prove (purify) you. God knows our infirmities, our weakness and will allow the trying to process us for Purpose. Because the purpose for Peter's life was so great, he could not operate in unbelief, doubt and fear. These all come to strip us, sift us of our power and authority. Jesus prayed that Peter would operate in the revelation that he had received and utilize his keys. Jesus knew that Peter already possessed the weapons needed to overcome, but Peter had to know how to use them and this was his opportunity. This was not just an attack, but this was an assignment. God was in control and allowed Peter to be set up, to perfect that, which was lacking in his faith. A fiery trial to get out all his imperfections, that he and his faith may be made whole. Peter had that same power and authority but had not tapped into it. We must know who Jesus is, who we are and the power and authority we have because of Him, to fulfill our purpose. All of life's challenges are designed to prove us: that we are eventually made in His likeness, for we must be like Him! God will always bring us face to face with our fears: that we may deal with them. It is then that we learn Who He Is. The weakness is only there that he might know who Jesus is. We have all got to know him for ourselves. We cannot allow fear of any kind to operate in our lives. It's like the yeast. **1 Cor 5:6** Your glorying is not good. Know ye not that a little leaven leaveneth the whole lump? If fear is allowed in one area, it will eventually spread to other areas. If we allow the enemy an inch, he will take us for a mile. We must be made perfect in love. **1 John 4:18** There is no fear in love; but perfect love casteth out fear: because fear hath torment. He that feareth is not made perfect in love.

Gone With The Wind!

The storm came to bless you.
John 3:8 Matt. 14:24-32

John 3:8

The wind bloweth where it listeth, and thou hearest the sound thereof, but canst not tell whence it cometh, and whither it goeth: so is every one that is born of the Spirit.

Every man that is born of the spirit does not know where he's going. It is the Spirit of God that leads him. Because God knows all things, wherever he leads you, just know that he knows the way. And because God is a Spirit, they that worship Him must worship Him in spirit and in truth.

Worship is to become one **with, or to be united with the Father.**

John 15:7 If ye abide in me (in my word), and my words abide in you,(we become one) ye shall ask what ye will, and it shall be done unto you.

John 1:1

In the beginning was the Word, and the Word was with God, and the Word was God.

John 1:14

And the Word was made flesh, and dwelt among us, (and we beheld his glory, the glory as of the only begotten of the Father,) full of grace and truth. God is his word and when we "come", we unite with or become one with Him. When we enter into agreement with God's word, it becomes flesh. We are the walking word. 2 Cor 3:2

Ye are our epistle written in our hearts, known and read of all men:

Wind is symbolic to Spirit.

Matt 14:2-32

4 But the ship was now in the midst of the sea, tossed with waves: for the wind was contrary.

25 And in the fourth watch of the night Jesus went unto them, walking on the sea.

26 And when the disciples saw him walking on the sea, they were troubled, saying, It is a spirit; and they cried out for fear.

27 But straightway Jesus spake unto them, saying, Be of good cheer; it is I; be not afraid.

28 And Peter answered him and said, Lord, if it be thou, bid me come unto thee on the water.

29 And he said, Come. And when Peter was come down out of the ship, he walked on the water, to go to Jesus.

30 But when he saw the wind boisterous, he was afraid; and beginning to sink, he cried, saying, Lord, save me.

31 And immediately Jesus stretched forth his hand, and caught him, and said unto him, O thou of little faith, wherefore didst thou doubt?

32 And when they were come into the ship, the wind ceased.

Matt 14:22-23

22 And straightway Jesus constrained his disciples to get into a ship, and to go before him unto the other side, while he sent the multitudes away.

23 And when he had sent the multitudes away, he went up into a mountain apart to pray: and when the evening was come, he was there alone.

24 But the ship was now in the midst of the sea, tossed with waves: for the wind was contrary. When we step out to obey God, we should expect opposition (storms). Anything that is contrary to what God tells to do is opposition. Often our journey starts out smooth but this story lets me

know that about half way, we can expect opposition. When we are so far out there, that we can't see anything but water. There is land nowhere in view, and now things get shaky. But remember who told you to go.

25 And in the fourth watch of the night Jesus went unto them, walking on the sea.

26 And when the disciples saw him walking on the sea, they were troubled, saying, It is a spirit; and they cried out for fear. Apparently these men did not see what they thought they saw. For if they had truly saw him, they would have not responded in fear. Seeing is believing. It is very important that you see clearly when in a storm. It's how you see a situation that determines how you respond to it. The answer to your problem is just that you need to see your way out. This is why Jesus told Nicodemus that you must be able to see the Kingdom of God to Enter the Kingdom of God. John 3:3,5 Jesus answered and said unto him, Verily, verily, I say unto thee, Except a man be born again, he cannot see the kingdom of God. Jesus answered, Verily, verily, I say unto thee, Except a man be born of water and of the Spirit, he cannot enter into the kingdom of God. If we can see our way, then we can walk it out. To see is to understand. God opens the eyes of our understanding, Spiritually, giving insight. That the God of our Lord Jesus Christ, the Father of glory, may give unto you the spirit of wisdom and revelation in the knowledge of him: The eyes of your understanding being enlightened; that ye may know what is the hope of his calling, and what is the riches of his glory of his inheritance in the saints. **Eph. 1: 17-18**

27 But straightway Jesus spake unto them, saying, Be of good cheer; it is I; be not afraid. As soon as Jesus recognize their fear, He manifests himself, by speaking. No matter how boisterous the situation gets, we must be able to see Jesus in the midst of it. If Jesus can't be seen, then it's probably because he didn't instruct you to do it.

28 And Peter answered him and said, Lord, if it be thou, bid me come unto thee (unite with thee) on the water.

29 And he said, Come. And when Peter was come (not came) down out of the ship, he walked on the water, to go to Jesus. Peter was come, Peter was

One, Peter was united, Peter was in worship, and they both were walking on the water.

30 But when he saw the wind boisterous, he was afraid; and beginning to sink, he cried, saying, Lord, save me. Remember it's all in what and how you see. Peter lost FOCUS. He took his eyes off Jesus, the word, fear set in and he began to sink. Just as we do when in a storm. We don't see Jesus in the midst at first because we are in our flesh. But when we get in the Spirit, then we are enlightened, that we are able to see Jesus. We have to stay in the Spirit to keep our eyes on Jesus (the word). Whatever word was spoken to us when we were called out, we must focus on that word. Whatever word is spoken to us when the opposition arises, and it will arise, we are to keep our eyes on that word. It is the word of God that keeps our focus on him, that we might learn, get to know, become INTIMATE, worship him.

Matt 11:28-30

Come unto me,(unite, worship) all ye that labour and are heavy laden, and I will give you rest.

29 Take my yoke upon you, and learn of me; for I am meek and lowly in heart: and ye shall find rest unto your souls.

30 For my yoke is easy, and my burden is light. Let God have the opposition and you take the word.

31 And immediately Jesus stretched forth his hand, and caught him, and said unto him, O thou of little faith, wherefore didst thou doubt? When Peter doubted, fear came in to distract him and turned his focus on the situation. God will not let you fall; it's only a test. Just like when teaching toddlers to walk. We're right there to catch them if they need us.

32 And when they were come into the ship, the wind ceased. Now they have become one with the ship. This is a place of comfort for Peter. Peter is in the ship and the ship was in Peter. In Peter's mind was the thought the ship can hold me and keep me safe, cause Jesus is on board. Why is it that we can only trust God through tangible means? Oh, we can have

great faith and trust God to keep us safe as long as we have a job, or as long as we have a man or woman. But don't be fooled. This is not faith at all. Faith is believing and trusting that God **will,** when there is nothing to work with. Knowing that His word is enough. That's faith!

The wind ceased cause Peter didn't need the Spirit to do what he could do naturally. Peter didn't know that the storm came to bless him. The storm came to give him the ability to supernaturally do what he couldn't do in the natural. It was his enabling power, but he didn't **see** it. It came that he might press in!

Acts 2:1-4

And when the day of Pentecost was fully come, they were all **with** one accord in one place. With the Spirit; worship, unity, oneness

2 And suddenly there came a sound from heaven as of a **rushing mighty wind**, and it filled all the house where they were sitting.

3 And there appeared unto them cloven tongues like as of fire, and it sat upon each of them.

4 And they were all filled with the Holy Ghost, and began to speak with other tongues, as the Spirit gave them utterance. Empowered to speak a language other than their natural or native language. When they became one with the Spirit, word, then the wind came. Whenever we become one with the word, Spirit of God, we are Prophesying and we should expect something to happen. But the wind must first come.

Ezek 37:1-10

The hand of the LORD was upon me, and carried me out in the spirit of the LORD, and set me down in the midst of the valley which was full of bones,

2 And caused me to pass by them round about: and, behold, there were very many in the open valley; and, lo, they were very dry.

3 And he said unto me, Son of man, can these bones live? And I answered, O Lord GOD, thou knowest.

4 Again he said unto me, Prophesy upon these bones, and say unto them, O ye dry bones, hear the word of the LORD.

5 Thus saith the Lord GOD unto these bones; Behold, I will cause breath to enter into you, and ye shall live:

6 And I will lay sinews upon you, and will bring up flesh upon you, and cover you with skin, and put breath in you, and ye shall live; and ye shall know that I am the LORD.

7 So I prophesied as I was commanded: (worshipped, united, became one with) and as I prophesied, there was a noise, and behold a shaking, and the bones came together, bone to his bone.

8 And when I beheld, lo, the sinews and the flesh came up upon them, and the skin covered them above: (exactly what God said would happen) but there was no breath in them. First the natural, then the spiritual.

9 Then said he unto me, Prophesy unto the **wind** (Spirit) prophesy, son of man, and say to the wind,(Spirit) Thus saith the Lord GOD; **Come** from the four winds, O breath, and breathe upon these slain, that they may live.

10 So I prophesied as he commanded me **(worshipped, united, onness)**, and the breath came into them, and they lived. **Life is in the Spirit)** and stood up upon their feet, an exceeding great army.

When Jesus said to Peter "Come" and Peter "was Come", Peter was worshipping, intimate, united, and One with Jesus. So there is no reason that he could not do what Jesus was doing.

Ex 14:13-16

13 And Moses said unto the people, Fear ye not, stand still, and see the salvation of the LORD, which he will shew to you to day: for the Egyptians whom ye have seen to day, ye shall see them again no more for ever.

14 The LORD shall fight for you, and ye shall hold your peace. The word fights for us and when we speak or send the word, we are send God. Knowing this enables us to hold on to our peace. Our peace is a sign that we really do believe and trust God.

15 And the LORD said unto Moses, Wherefore criest thou unto me? speak unto the children of Israel, that they **go forward:**

16 But lift thou up thy rod,(word) and stretch out thine hand over the sea, and divide it: and the children of Israel shall go on dry ground through the midst of the sea.

God created a valley, but the valley was caused by the wind. Ps 23:4

Yea, though I walk through the valley of the shadow of death, I will fear no evil: for thou art with me; thy rod (word) and thy staff (word) they comfort me.

Ex 14:21-22

21 And Moses stretched out his hand over the sea and the LORD caused the sea to go back by a strong east wind all that night, and made the sea dry land, and the waters were divided. Oneness, unity, worship- (Obedience) Caused the wind to come. The storm came to bless them.

22 And the children of Israel went into the midst of the sea upon the dry ground: and the waters were a wall unto them on their right hand, and on their left.

Ex 15:9-10 The Lord flip the script on the enemy in the wind

9 The enemy said, I will pursue, I will overtake, I will divide the spoil; my lust shall be satisfied upon them; I will draw my sword, my hand shall destroy them.

10 Thou didst blow with thy wind, the sea covered them: they sank as lead in the mighty waters.

When Jesus said to Peter come and Peter was come, he prophesied with his actions. When God told Ezekiel to prophesy to the four winds to come and he said four winds come. When God told Moses to stretch forth thy hand over the sea and divide it, Moses stretched forth his hand over the sea and the God, (word) caused the wind to come and roll back the sea.

The storm is coming out of your mouth, to give you supernatural strength and power that propels you to the place God wants to get you to. It doesn't matter if God is causing the wind or if God is allowing the wind, just know it's working for your good.

We Must Realize:

1. **We must keep our eyes on the word.**
2. **The storm is coming out of our mouth.**
3. **The wind is there to assist me in getting to where God is taking me.** (Be not afraid, God is in control)
4. **The storm came to bless me.**

We Must Recognize:

1. **God's in the midst, be not afraid.**
2. **I can't doubt, it leads to fear.**
3. **When we speak the word of God, We are prophesying, becoming one, united with God and we must expect the wind to come.**
4. **The wind comes to supernaturally propel me to where God is taking me.** (to the other side)
5. **It came to bless me!**

The Glory of the Valley

Ps 23:1-4

The LORD is my shepherd; I shall not want.

2 He maketh me to lie down in green pastures: he leadeth me beside the still waters.

3 He restoreth my soul: he leadeth me in the paths of righteousness for his name's sake.

4 Yea, though I walk through the valley of the shadow of death, I will fear no evil: for thou art with me; thy rod and thy staff they comfort me.

I Shepherd – One who takes care of sheep, to lead, feed and protect. One who watches over carefully and guides those who believe in him and put their trust in him.

John 10:1-5

Verily, verily, I say unto you, He that entereth not by the door into the sheepfold, but climbeth up some other way, the same is a thief and a robber.

2 But he that entereth in by the door is the shepherd of the sheep.

3 To him the porter openeth; and the sheep hear his voice: and he calleth his own sheep by name, and leadeth them out.

4 And when he putteth forth his own sheep, he goeth before them, and the sheep follow him: for they know his voice.

5 And a stranger will they not follow, but will flee from him: for they know not the voice of strangers. **The good Shepherd lays down his life.**

John 10:9

I am the door: by me if any man (**sheep**) enter in, he shall be saved, and shall go in and out, and find pasture.

Jer 29:11

11 For I know the thoughts that I think toward you, saith the LORD, thoughts of peace, and not of evil, to give you an expected end. **The Shepherd has the plan.**

Job 23:10

10 But he knoweth the way that I take: when he hath tried me, I shall come forth as gold.

He knows the way.

Isa 48:17

17 Thus saith the LORD, thy Redeemer, the Holy One of Israel; I am the LORD thy God which teacheth thee to profit, which leadeth thee by the way that thou shouldest go. **He instructs and teaches in the way that He has chosen.**

II **I shall not want** – like a Father there to provide and protect, supplying all my needs. **Ps 34:9-10** fear the LORD, ye his saints: for there is no want to them that fear him.

10 The young lions do lack, and suffer hunger: but they that seek the LORD shall not want any good thing.

III **Lie down (Rest) in green pastures, abundant provision, prosperity, harvest. Eph 3:20** Now unto him that is able to do exceeding abundantly above all that we ask or think, according to the power that worketh in us, **Still waters** – fulfilling, satisfying, my thirst and desires in a place of peace, calmness, **Jer 31:3** The LORD hath appeared of old unto me, saying, Yea, I have loved thee with an everlasting love: therefore with lovingkindness have I drawn thee. God knows how to lure us into a place! All pleasing to the flesh, all in good times. Like a fisherman setting his nets, preparing for a haul.

IV **Restores my soul** – **bring back to original condition or place. John 17:5**

And now, O Father, glorify thou me with thine own self with the glory which I had with thee before the world was. Back to a place of oneness, worship, before contamination, sin entered in.

John 1:1-2

In the beginning was the Word, and the Word was with God, and the Word was God.

2 The same was in the beginning with God.

John 1:13-14

13 Which were born, not of blood, nor of the will of the flesh, nor of the will of man, but of God.

14 And the Word was made flesh, and dwelt among us, (and we beheld his glory, the glory as of the only begotten of the Father,) full of grace and truth. Not born of flesh, but of the will of the Father.

Restores through the pressures of life, my soul – mind, will, emotions, intellect, and imagination.

My mind – when it seems all hope is gone and looks like no way out and I can't figure it out! **Ps 25:12-13** What man is he that feareth the LORD? him shall he teach in the way that he shall choose.

13 His soul shall dwell at ease; and his seed shall inherit the earth. **Restores my soul**

My will - When I can't do what I desire to do, cause what I desire not to do has a holt on me that I just can't seem to shake. It's holding me against my will

Rom 7:20-24 Now if I do that I would not, it is no more I that do it, but sin that dwelleth in me.

21 I find then a law, that, when I would do good, evil is present with me.

22 For I delight in the law of God after the inward man:

23 But I see another law in my members, warring against the law of my mind, and bringing me into captivity to the law of sin which is in my members.

24 O wretched man that I am! who shall deliver me from the body of this death?

Restores my soul

My emotions - When my spirit is in an uproar, happy one minute and sad the next. Today I'm in and tomorrow I'm out; confused, depressed, weary and no rest. Frustrated, constipated, laughing on the outside and crying on the inside. Riding the roller coaster of life. **John 16:33** These things I have spoken unto you, that in me ye might have peace. In the world ye shall have tribulation: but be of good cheer; I have overcome the world. **II Cor 4:7-10** But we have this treasure in earthen vessels, that the excellency of the power may be of God, and not of us.

8 We are troubled on every side, yet not distressed; we are perplexed, but not in despair;

9 Persecuted, but not forsaken; cast down, but not destroyed;

10 Always bearing about in the body the dying of the Lord Jesus, that the life also of Jesus might be made manifest in our body. **Restores my soul**

My intellect – When I don't know who I am, scared from another man's words, opinions and frustrations: unable to be me. Bound and not free, dictating to how others perceive me to be. **Rom 8:31** What shall we then say to these things? If God be for us, who can be against us?

Rom 8:35-39

35 Who shall separate us from the love of Christ? shall tribulation, or distress, or persecution, or famine, or nakedness, or peril, or sword?

36 As it is written, For thy sake we are killed all the day long; we are accounted as sheep for the slaughter.

37 Nay, in all these things we are more than conquerors through him that loved us.

38 For I am persuaded, that neither death, nor life, nor angels, nor principalities, nor powers, nor things present, nor things to come,

39 Nor height, nor depth, nor any other creature, shall be able to separate us from the love of God, which is in Christ Jesus our Lord.

1 Peter 3:13

13 And who is he that will harm you, if ye be followers of that which is good?

My imagination – When I can't break free from the pictures in my mind. From all the negative thinking, what could, would or what should have happen based on my opinion and the opinion of others.

Isa 54:17

No weapon that is formed against thee shall prosper; and every tongue that shall rise against thee in judgment thou shalt condemn. This is the heritage of the servants of the LORD, and their righteousness is of me, saith the LORD.

Isa 50:8-9

He is near that justifieth me; who will contend with me? let us stand together: who is mine adversary? let him come near to me.

9 Behold, the Lord GOD will help me; who is he that shall condemn me? lo, they all shall wax old as a garment; the moth shall eat them up. He will contend for me.

Phil 1:20

According to my earnest expectation and my hope, that in nothing I shall be ashamed, but that with all boldness, as always, so now also Christ shall be magnified in my body, **whether it be by life, or by death.** Restores my soul.

Bringing me to a place of Oneness, a place of Worship.

V He leadeth me in the Path of Righteousness, Ps 25:4-5,10

Shew me thy ways, O LORD; teach me thy paths.

5 Lead me in thy truth, and teach me: for thou art the God of my salvation; on thee do I wait all the day.

10 All the paths of the LORD are mercy and truth unto such as keep his covenant and his testimonies.

Ps 37:23

The steps of a good man are ordered by the LORD: and he delighteth in his way.

Matt 7:13-14

Enter ye in at the strait gate: for wide is the gate, and broad is the way, that leadeth to destruction, and many there be which go in thereat:

14 Because strait is the gate, and narrow is the way, which leadeth unto life, and few there be that find it.

For His name's sake - 1 Peter 2:9 But ye are a chosen generation, a royal priesthood, an holy nation, a peculiar people; that ye should shew forth the praises of him who hath called you out of darkness into his marvellous light: To show forth the praise of His glory!

Eph 1:17-20

That the God of our Lord Jesus Christ, the Father of glory, may give unto you the spirit of wisdom and revelation in the knowledge of him:

18 The eyes of your understanding being enlightened; that ye may know what is the hope of his calling, and what the riches of the glory of his inheritance in the saints,

19 And what is the exceeding greatness of his power to usward who believe, according to the working of his mighty power,

20 Which he wrought in Christ, when he raised him from the dead, and set him at his own right hand in the heavenly places, His inheritance. That he might receive a withdrawal with interest, to the deposit or investment that he has made in us.

VI Yea though I walk through the valley of the shadow of Death.

Prov 12:28

28 In the way of righteousness is life; and in the pathway thereof there is no death.

John 12:24-26

Verily, verily, I say unto you, Except a corn of wheat fall into the ground and die, it abideth alone: but if it die, it bringeth forth much fruit.

25 He that loveth his life shall lose it; and he that hateth his life in this world shall keep it unto life eternal. We don't die, we multiply!

John 17:24-26

Father, I will that they also, whom thou hast given me, be with me where I am; that they may behold my glory, which thou hast given me: for thou lovedst me before the foundation of the world.

26 If any man serve me, let him **follow** me; and where I am, there shall also my servant be: if any man serve me, him will my Father honour. The safest place is where Jesus is. It's not good to be on the mountain, when Jesus is in the valley.

I will fear no evil, For thou art with me.

I am, is with you, I am is leading you, I am is going before you! No need to fear when I am, that I am, is near.

Yea = Yes. Jesus walked through a valley but it began with a YES! Mark 14:36

And he said, Abba, Father, all things are possible unto thee; take away this cup from me: nevertheless not what I will, but what thou wilt. YES

Restoring my soul brought me back to a place of oneness with the shepherd, empowering (equipping) me to walk through the valley!

Walk through – Constant progress or movement.

The Process: Valley – A stretch of flat low land between hills or mountains, often with a running river through it. A place of humility flowing with life, which explains why it is a shadow of death. Where there is water, there is life. We cannot live where there is no water.

John 4:13-14

13 Jesus answered and said unto her, Whosoever drinketh of this water shall thirst again:

14 But whosoever drinketh of the water that I shall give him shall never thirst; but the water that I shall give him shall be in him a well of water springing up into everlasting life.

John 7:37-38

In the last day, that great day of the feast, Jesus stood and cried, saying, If any man thirst, let him come unto me.

38 He that believeth on me, as the scripture hath said, out of his belly shall flow rivers of living water.

"I Will Fear No Evil"! Now our will is the Father's will. We be one!

John 17:20-24

20 Neither pray I for these alone, but for them also which shall believe on me through their word;

21 That they all may be one; as thou, Father, art in me, and I in thee, that they also may be one in us: that the world may believe that thou hast sent me.

22 And the glory which thou gavest me I have given them; that they may be one, even as we are one:

23 I in them, and thou in me, that they may be made perfect in one; and that the world may know that thou hast sent me, and hast loved them, as thou hast loved me.

24 Father, I will that they also, whom thou hast given me, be with me where I am; that they may behold my glory, which thou hast given me: for thou lovedst me before the foundation of the world.

When we become one with the Jesus, the Father, the word, the living water, there is no room for evil, no room for fear!

True Intimacy Is Birthed In The Valley! Jesus walked through that valley, from judgement hall to judgement hall, to a place called Golgotha, where he faced the Mount of Calvary.

John 18-19

When Jesus had spoken these words, he went forth with his disciples over the brook Cedron, where was a garden, into the which he entered, and his disciples.

2 And Judas also, which betrayed him, knew the place: for Jesus ofttimes resorted thither with his disciples.

3 Judas then, having received a band of men and officers from the chief priests and Pharisees, cometh thither with lanterns and torches and weapons.

4 Jesus therefore, knowing all things that should come upon him, went forth, and said unto them, Whom seek ye?

5 They answered him, Jesus of Nazareth. Jesus saith unto them, I am he. And Judas also, which betrayed him, stood with them.

6 As soon then as he had said unto them, I am he, they went backward, and fell to the ground.

7 Then asked he them again, Whom seek ye? And they said, Jesus of Nazareth.

8 Jesus answered, I have told you that I am he: if therefore ye seek me, let these go their way:

9 That the saying might be fulfilled, which he spake, Of them which thou gavest me have I lost none.

10 Then Simon Peter having a sword drew it, and smote the high priest's servant, and cut off his right ear. The servant's name was Malchus.

11 Then said Jesus unto Peter, Put up thy sword into the sheath: the cup which my Father hath given me, shall I not drink it?

12 Then the band and the captain and officers of the Jews took Jesus, and bound him,

13 And led him away to Annas first; for he was father in law to Caiaphas, which was the high priest that same year.

14 Now Caiaphas was he, which gave counsel to the Jews, that it was expedient that one man should die for the people.

15 And Simon Peter followed Jesus, and so did another disciple: that disciple was known unto the high priest, and went in with Jesus into the palace of the high priest.

16 But Peter stood at the door without. Then went out that other disciple, which was known unto the high priest, and spake unto her that kept the door, and brought in Peter.

17 Then saith the damsel that kept the door unto Peter, Art not thou also one of this man's disciples? He saith, I am not.

18 And the servants and officers stood there, who had made a fire of coals; for it was cold: and they warmed themselves: and Peter stood with them, and warmed himself.

19 The high priest then asked Jesus of his disciples, and of his doctrine.

20 Jesus answered him, I spake openly to the world; I ever taught in the synagogue, and in the temple, whither the Jews always resort; and in secret have I said nothing.

21 Why askest thou me? ask them which heard me, what I have said unto them: behold, they know what I said.

22 And when he had thus spoken, one of the officers which stood by struck Jesus with the palm of his hand, saying, Answerest thou the high priest so?

23 Jesus answered him, If I have spoken evil, bear witness of the evil: but if well, why smitest thou me?

24 Now Annas had sent him bound unto Caiaphas the high priest.

25 And Simon Peter stood and warmed himself. They said therefore unto him, Art not thou also one of his disciples? He denied it, and said, I am not.

26 One of the servants of the high priest, being his kinsman whose ear Peter cut off, saith, Did not I see thee in the garden with him?

27 Peter then denied again: and immediately the cock crew.

28 Then led they Jesus from Caiaphas unto the hall of judgment: and it was early; and they themselves went not into the judgment hall, lest they should be defiled; but that they might eat the passover.

29 Pilate then went out unto them, and said, What accusation bring ye against this man?

30 They answered and said unto him, If he were not a malefactor, we would not have delivered him up unto thee.

31 Then said Pilate unto them, Take ye him, and judge him according to your law. The Jews therefore said unto him, It is not lawful for us to put any man to death:

32 That the saying of Jesus might be fulfilled, which he spake, signifying what death he should die.

33 Then Pilate entered into the judgment hall again, and called Jesus, and said unto him, Art thou the King of the Jews?

34 Jesus answered him, Sayest thou this thing of thyself, or did others tell it thee of me?

35 Pilate answered, Am I a Jew? Thine own nation and the chief priests have delivered thee unto me: what hast thou done?

36 Jesus answered, My kingdom is not of this world: if my kingdom were of this world, then would my servants fight, that I should not be delivered to the Jews: but now is my kingdom not from hence.

37 Pilate therefore said unto him, Art thou a king then? Jesus answered, Thou sayest that I am a king. To this end was I born, and for this cause came I into the world, that I should bear witness unto the truth. Every one that is of the truth heareth my voice.

38 Pilate saith unto him, What is truth? And when he had said this, he went out again unto the Jews, and saith unto them, I find in him no fault at all.

39 But ye have a custom, that I should release unto you one at the passover: will ye therefore that I release unto you the King of the Jews?

40 Then cried they all again, saying, Not this man, but Barabbas. Now Barabbas was a robber.

John 19

Then Pilate therefore took Jesus, and scourged him.

2 And the soldiers platted a crown of thorns, and put it on his head, and they put on him a purple robe,

3 And said, Hail, King of the Jews! and they smote him with their hands.

4 Pilate therefore went forth again, and saith unto them, Behold, I bring him forth to you, that ye may know that I find no fault in him.

5 Then came Jesus forth, wearing the crown of thorns, and the purple robe. And Pilate saith unto them, Behold the man!

6 When the chief priests therefore and officers saw him, they cried out, saying, Crucify him, crucify him. Pilate saith unto them, Take ye him, and crucify him: for I find no fault in him.

7 The Jews answered him, We have a law, and by our law he ought to die, because he made himself the Son of God.

8 When Pilate therefore heard that saying, he was the more afraid;

9 And went again into the judgment hall, and saith unto Jesus, Whence art thou? But Jesus gave him no answer.

10 Then saith Pilate unto him, Speakest thou not unto me? knowest thou not that I have power to crucify thee, and have power to release thee?

11 Jesus answered, Thou couldest have no power at all against me, except it were given thee from above: therefore he that delivered me unto thee hath the greater sin.

12 And from thenceforth Pilate sought to release him: but the Jews cried out, saying, If thou let this man go, thou art not Caesar's friend: whosoever maketh himself a king speaketh against Caesar.

13 When Pilate therefore heard that saying, he brought Jesus forth, and sat down in the judgment seat in a place that is called the Pavement, but in the Hebrew, Gabbatha.

14 And it was the preparation of the passover, and about the sixth hour: and he saith unto the Jews, Behold your King!

15 But they cried out, Away with him, away with him, crucify him. Pilate saith unto them, Shall I crucify your King? The chief priest answered, We have no king but Caesar.

16 Then delivered he him therefore unto them to be crucified. And they took Jesus, and led him away.

17 And he bearing his cross went forth into a place called the place of a skull, which is called in the Hebrew Golgotha:

18 Where they crucified him, and two other with him, on either side one, and Jesus in the midst.

19 And Pilate wrote a title, and put it on the cross. And the writing was, JESUS OF NAZARETH THE KING OF THE JEWS.

20 This title then read many of the Jews: for the place where Jesus was crucified was nigh to the city: and it was written in Hebrew, and Greek, and Latin.

21 Then said the chief priests of the Jews to Pilate, Write not, The King of the Jews; but that he said, I am King of the Jews.

22 Pilate answered, What I have written I have written.

23 Then the soldiers, when they had crucified Jesus, took his garments, and made four parts, to every soldier a part; and also his coat: now the coat was without seam, woven from the top throughout.

24 They said therefore among themselves, Let us not rend it, but cast lots for it, whose it shall be: that the scripture might be fulfilled, which saith, They parted my raiment among them, and for my vesture they did cast lots. These things therefore the soldiers did.

25 Now there stood by the cross of Jesus his mother, and his mother's sister, Mary the wife of Cleophas, and Mary Magdalene.

26 When Jesus therefore saw his mother, and the disciple standing by, whom he loved, he saith unto his mother, Woman, behold thy son!

27 Then saith he to the disciple, Behold thy mother! And from that hour that disciple took her unto his own home.

28 After this, Jesus knowing that all things were now accomplished, that the scripture might be fulfilled, saith, I thirst.

29 Now there was set a vessel full of vinegar: and they filled a spunge with vinegar, and put it upon hyssop, and put it to his mouth.

30 When Jesus therefore had received the vinegar, he said, It is finished: and he bowed his head, and gave up the ghost.

31 The Jews therefore, because it was the preparation, that the bodies should not remain upon the cross on the sabbath day, (for that sabbath day was an high day,) besought Pilate that their legs might be broken, and that they might be taken away.

32 Then came the soldiers, and brake the legs of the first, and of the other which was crucified with him.

33 But when they came to Jesus, and saw that he was dead already, they brake not his legs:

34 But one of the soldiers with a spear pierced his side, and forthwith came there out blood and water.

35 And he that saw it bare record, and his record is true: and he knoweth that he saith true, that ye might believe.

36 For these things were done, that the scripture should be fulfilled, A bone of him shall not be broken.

37 And again another scripture saith, They shall look on him whom they pierced.

38 And after this Joseph of Arimathaea, being a disciple of Jesus, but secretly for fear of the Jews, besought Pilate that he might take away the body of Jesus: and Pilate gave him leave. He came therefore, and took the body of Jesus.

39 And there came also Nicodemus, which at the first came to Jesus by night, and brought a mixture of myrrh and aloes, about an hundred pound weight.

40 Then took they the body of Jesus, and wound it in linen clothes with the spices, as the manner of the Jews is to bury.

41 Now in the place where he was crucified there was a garden; and in the garden a new sepulchre, wherein was never man yet laid.

42 There laid they Jesus therefore because of the Jews' preparation day; for the sepulchre was nigh at hand.

Because Jesus was the word that became flesh, He could not return void, He had to abide forever. **Isa 40:8** The grass withereth, the flower fadeth: but the word of our God shall stand for ever. So death was only a shadow!

When we become one with the Father, the word, we enter into covenant and we can not die, therefore it's not what it looks like. In covenant, the word, His strength is exchanged for or made perfect in our weakness. The shepherd restores our soul, to prepare us to walk through the valley, which takes us to a place of victory (purpose).

This is why our enemies have to be fought in the valley, because the enemy can not drink or partake of the water in which we drink, For it is only given to those of Covenant. Therefore he will die in the valley.

Mountain	Mountain
David	Goliath

Valley of the shadow of Death

Covenant	Armour
Of the Blood,	
Word	

Both were strong on the mountain. Israel had to come out of Egypt to defeat Pharoah. You can not conquer nor change what you conform to. The battle is won when the enemy feels that he has the advantage over you in your weakness. As long as you are in your strength or place of comfort, God's strength (glory) will not be seen.

1 Cor 1:29 That no flesh should glory in his presence. Flesh can not survive in the valley.

IV

The Prize

I press toward the mark for the prize of the high calling of God in Christ Jesus.

Phil 3:14

Heaven On Earth

Matt 6:10 Thy kingdom come. Thy will be done in earth, as it is in heaven.

1 Peter 1:1-16

Peter writing about submission, God's divine order and most of all suffering, conceals a hidden treasure. Blessings are often hidden in trials and sufferings. No matter what the situation may be God always rewards those who are faithful to obey and endure until the end. **Eccl 3:1** To every thing there is a season, and a time to every purpose under the heaven: **Heb 10:36** For ye have need of patience, that, after ye have done the will of God, ye might receive the promise. Peter focuses his attention on a body of believers who were persecuted for their beliefs and scattered. **1 Peter 1:1** Peter, an apostle of Jesus Christ, to the strangers scattered throughout Pontus, Galatia, Cappadocia, Asia, and Bithynia, This persecution that was designed to stop the spread of the gospel, assisted in multiplying the number of believers. **Acts 1:1-4** The former treatise have I made, O Theophilus, of all that Jesus began both to do and teach,

2 Until the day in which he was taken up, after that he through the Holy Ghost had given commandments unto the apostles whom he had chosen:

3 To whom also he shewed himself alive after his passion by many infallible proofs, being seen of them forty days, and speaking of the things pertaining to the kingdom of God:

4 And, being assembled together with them, commanded them that they should not depart from Jerusalem, but wait for the promise of the Father, which, saith he, ye have heard of me.

God always takes what the enemy means for bad and works it for the good. No matter what we go through, if we only stay faithful to obey, then God gets the glory.

A body of believers **Chosen- according to the fore knowledge of God the Father.

Chosen- hand picked, **Jer 1:5 Before I formed thee in the belly I knew thee; and before thou camest forth out of the womb I sanctified thee, and I ordained thee a prophet unto the nations. Hand picked according to fore knowledge of you and your purpose, through sanctification. The act of being set apart for the work of the Spirit.

2 Elect according to the foreknowledge of God the Father, through sanctification of the Spirit, unto obedience and sprinkling of the blood of Jesus Christ: Grace unto you, and peace, be multiplied. Unto obedience and sprinkling of the blood of Jesus Christ and submission of authority (order) and holiness. God has chosen us and set us apart for His work, that we should obey authority and be holy. Ps 24:3-4

3 Who shall ascend into the hill of the LORD? or who shall stand in his holy place?4 He that hath clean hands, and a pure heart; who hath not lifted up his soul unto vanity, nor sworn deceitfully. Grace unto you (favor) and peace be multiplied.

3 Blessed be the God and Father of our Lord Jesus Christ, which according to his abundant mercy hath begotten us again unto a lively hope by the resurrection of Jesus Christ from the dead, Begotten us again signified, a new birth, a spiritual birth; one that's alive and not dead. A new testament hope.

A new birth = A renewed mind, a new mind set. We can't go into Canaan with an Egypt mentality.

4 To an inheritance incorruptible, and undefiled, and that fadeth not away, reserved in heaven for you, * Inheritance – To receive as a legacy or promise to come into possession of or receive as a rightful heir. *A legacy, a promise, one that could only come through Jesus. God has chosen us, hand picked us, sanctified us, set us apart, for the work of His Spirit. And that we should obey authority and live holy. And because he knows that we have flaws he has allowed and abundance of mercy, giving us a new hope, one that's alive, because he has something for us, an inheritance.

*Incorruptible – that which can not decay and can not be corrupted morally, by man's hands, nor tarnish or decrease in value.

- Undefiled – pure, holy and righteous.
- Fadeth not away – always in the bank, there when you need it!
- Reserved – made reservation, holding for a special purpose, place and time.

In heaven for you on earth. **Ps 119:89** For ever, O LORD, thy word is settled in heaven. **Matt 18:20** For where two or three are gathered together in my name, there am I in the midst of them. So we must go up in the spirit and bring it down to earth. We must speak the heavenly language, not of this earth. **Phil 3:20** For our conversation is in heaven; from whence also we look for the Saviour, the Lord Jesus Christ:

5 Who are **kept** by the power of God through faith unto salvation ready to be revealed in the last time.

6 Wherein ye greatly rejoice, though now for a season, if need be, ye are in heaviness through manifold temptations: Those who have determined that quitting is not an option and that there is no looking back. Those who have decided to be and have what God has originally purposed. Those who have decided to forget press and to reach.

Phil 3:12-16 Not as though I had already attained, either were already perfect: but I follow after, if that I may apprehend that for which also I am apprehended of Christ Jesus. Not as though I had already arrived, either were already perfected, but I follow after, if that I may become (apprehend or hold to) that which I am also apprehended (chosen) of Christ.

13 Brethren, I count not myself to have apprehended: but this one thing I do, forgetting those things which are behind, and reaching forth unto those things which are before, I don't proclaim to have it all together, neither am I the sum total of what God says I am, but this one thing, all I know is one thing, I'm forgetting (choosing not to dwell on) those things which are behind.

14 I press toward the mark for the prize of the high calling of God in Christ Jesus. reaching forth (beyond self) for those things which are before (the prophesied place). To give it all I've got, toward the mark, the finish line. My focus is now before me, on the prize of the high calling (another dimension of faith) of God in Christ Jesus. I press to get to the place in which God is calling me to, living. giving, praying, fasting, commitment, sacrifice and integrity. My word must become my bond!

15 Let us therefore, as many as be perfect, be thus minded: and if in any thing ye be otherwise minded, God shall reveal even this unto you. Those who have made a conscience decision, not confused, unsure or unstable, but those who can say,

" That was then and this is now, I've been around that mountain long enough, it's now time to move upward! Upward! From faith to faith, to glory to glory!

The New Thing

"A New Glory" II Corn 3:7-11

7 But if the ministration of death, (the law) written and engraven in stones, was glorious, so that the children of Israel could not stedfastly behold the face of Moses for the glory of his countenance; which glory was to be done away: The glory is in the presence of the God. Moses went Upward to the place God had called him to. The place God had apprehended for him, (to get the law), which set a standard to teach the people of sin. This could not set the people free, but only bring forth bondage, (6) for the letter killeth but the spirit giveth life. Though this was the glory of God, it was temporary.

8 How shall not the ministration of the spirit be rather glorious?

9 For if the ministration of condemnation be glory, much more doth the ministration of righteousness exceed in glory. That which can only be done by the spirit, the hand of God, trusting God and doing what the spirit orders, exceeds in glory. **Eph 3:20** Now unto him that is able to do exceeding abundantly above all that we ask or think, **according to the power that worketh in us,** The power working in you is working while you Rest.

10 For even that which was made glorious had no glory in this respect, by reason of the glory that excelleth. That which we call glory has no glory in comparison to what God, by his spirit, is ready to reveal. **It's bigger than you think!** This glory is only a pattern of things to come.

Heb 9:1 Then verily the first covenant had also ordinances of divine service, and a worldly sanctuary. Even though the first glory was temporary, it was God's divine order, for that time.

Heb 9:6-9 Now when these things were thus ordained, the priests went always into the first tabernacle, accomplishing the service of God. Ordered by God, accomplishing a finished work, one that could only take them so far, with limitations. It had to be upgraded!

7 But into the second went the high priest alone once every year, not without blood, which he offered for himself, and for the errors of the people: It's better the second time around. The first Adam could only take us so far which led to death and bondage, but the second Adam, Christ Jesus brought life eternally.

8 The Holy Ghost this signifying, that the way into the holiest of all was not yet made manifest, while as the first tabernacle was yet standing: The Holy Ghost giving signs, that though you are here, it ain't where you are going to be. While you are here, I'm going to show you a better way. All in a process while the first was yet standing. God didn't tear it down and then build, it was at work at the same time (working through faith). Just as while He was stripping Saul of his kingdom, at the same time, He was yet raising up David. Preparing him to come forth at the time apprehended for him.(Reservations already made)

9 Which was a figure for the time then present, in which were offered both gifts and sacrifices, that could not make him that did the service perfect, as pertaining to the conscience; A figure or an image for that place and time. God's plan for that place and time allowed practices that he knew were not going to produce the outcome required, But it was his divine will, at that time. We must know the time in which we are in and what God desires and requires!

Heb 9:23-24 It was therefore necessary that the patterns of things in the heavens should be purified with these; but the heavenly things themselves with better sacrifices than these. The pattern allowed those sacrafices that did not bring about perfection, yet perfecting their faith. But heavenly things, the real deal, require better sacrafices. What use to work, don't work any more, **Come Up!**

24 For Christ is not entered into the holy places made with hands, which are the figures of the true; but into heaven itself, now to appear in the presence of God for us: It's bigger than man. It's God himself, his manifested presence, The glory cloud.

There must always be a pattern or blue print so to say!

** Blood of Goats   ** Blood of Jesus

** Abraham   ** God the Father

** Isaac   ** Jesus

** Joseph   ** Jesus

Isaiah 51:1-2

51:1 Hearken to me, ye that follow after righteousness, ye that seek the LORD: look unto the rock whence ye are hewn, and to the hole of the pit whence ye are digged.

2 Look unto Abraham your father, and unto Sarah that bare you: for I called him alone, and blessed him, and increased him. A pattern of God, but also a pattern of righteousness. Called out, apprehended of God for purpose.

Jesus on the Cross – you and I baring our cross

1 Peter 2:21 For even hereunto were ye called: because Christ also suffered for us, leaving us an example, that ye should follow his steps:

Isa 51:16 And I have put my words in thy mouth, and I have covered thee in the shadow of mine hand, that I may plant the heavens, and lay the foundations of the earth, and say unto Zion, Thou art my people. Heaven On Earth!

I Peter 1:7-13 That the trial of your faith, being much more precious than of gold that perisheth, though it be tried with fire, might be found unto praise and honour and glory at the appearing of Jesus Christ:

8 Whom having not seen, ye love; in whom, though now ye see him not, yet believing, ye rejoice with joy unspeakable and full of glory:

9 Receiving the end of your faith, even the salvation of your souls.

10 Of which salvation the prophets have inquired and searched diligently, who prophesied of the grace that should come unto you:

11 Searching what, or what manner of time the Spirit of Christ which was in them did signify, when it testified beforehand the sufferings of Christ, and the glory that should follow.

12 Unto whom it was revealed, that not unto themselves, but unto us they did minister the things, which are now reported unto you by them that have preached the gospel unto you with the Holy Ghost sent down from heaven; which things the angels desire to look into.

13 Wherefore gird up the loins of your mind, be sober, and hope to the end for the **grace** that is to be brought unto you at the **revelation** of Jesus Christ;

14 As obedient children, not fashioning yourselves according to the former lusts in your ignorance:

15 But as he which hath called you is holy, so be ye holy in all manner of conversation;

16 Because it is written, Be ye holy; for I am holy.

How to receive the end of your faith.

Isa 51:16 And I have put my words in thy mouth, and I have covered thee in the shadow of mine hand, that I may plant the heavens, and lay the foundations of the earth, and say unto Zion, Thou art my people. The word must be always coming forth out of your mouth. This can only be done if you sanctify the Lord God in your hearts: and be ready always to give an answer to every man that asketh you a reason of the hope that is in you with meekness and fear: 1 Peter 3:15 Oh generation of vipers, how can ye, being evil, speak good things? for out of the abundance of the heart the mouth speaketh. **Matt 12:34**

Then you must allow God to cover you in the shadow of his hand. You must Humble yourselves therefore under the mighty hand of God, that he may exalt you in due time: **1 Peter 5:6** and pray Thy kingdom come. Thy will be done in earth, as it is in heaven. **Matt 6:10**

I must be in the right place at the right time. Ex 33:13-23

13 Now therefore, I pray thee, if I have found grace in thy sight, shew me now thy way, that I may know thee, that I may find grace in thy sight: and consider that this nation is thy people.

14 And he said, My presence shall go with thee, and I will give thee rest.

15 And he said unto him, If thy presence go not with me, carry us not up hence.

16 For wherein shall it be known here that I and thy people have found grace in thy sight? is it not in that thou goest with us? so shall we be separated, I and thy people, from all the people that are upon the face of the earth.

17 And the LORD said unto Moses, I will do this thing also that thou hast spoken: for thou hast found grace in my sight, and I know thee by name.

18 And he said, I beseech thee, shew me thy glory.

19 And he said, I will make all my goodness pass before thee, and I will proclaim the name of the LORD before thee; and will be gracious to whom I will be gracious, and will shew mercy on whom I will shew mercy.

20 And he said, Thou canst not see my face: for there shall no man see me, and live.

21 And the LORD said, Behold, there is a place by me, and thou shalt stand upon a rock: God's will, the blessing is predicated on you being in the right place connected to the right man with the blessing.

Rock = Revelation Of Christ Kingdom

22 And it shall come to pass, while my glory passeth by, that I will put thee in a clift of the rock, (place of revelation) and will cover thee with my hand (the place of humility) while I pass by:

23 And I will take away mine hand, and thou shalt see my back parts: but my face shall not be seen. In a place where the enemy can't touch you.

Matt 16:18-19

18 And I say also unto thee, That thou art Peter, and upon this rock, revelation, I will build my church**; and the gates of hell shall not prevail against it.**

19 And I will give unto thee the keys of the kingdom of heaven: and whatsoever thou shalt bind on earth shall be bound in heaven: and whatsoever thou shalt loose on earth shall be loosed in heaven. Ex. 33:22, **while-** all at the same time, the glory is passing. His shadow will be a shield on the left, right, front and back; compassing you about with favor as a shield. **Ps. 5:12** God says, " I will put in the cleft of the rock, the place of revelation, and I will cover thee width my hand, while I pass by. While I'm covering you with my hand, all you got to do is stay under there, humbling yourself and at the proper time I will exhalt you. Once I've passed by and you can no longer see my face, I will show you my back.

I'm reminded of Star Trek. Whenever they got ready to get transported, they had to always get to a certain place, a certain position, in confidence and speak the language or password. The word always came from the captain and they always left with a smile of their faces. So it is with God.

1. **Position -** We must be in God's divine will. There in his presence, power, provisions.
2. **We must get the Revelation** – We must have an intimate relationship with him. We must get in the place of revelation and stay there. This is the only way we can **1 Peter 1:13** Wherefore gird up the loins of your mind, be sober, and hope to the end for the **grace** that is to be brought unto you at the **revelation** of Jesus Christ; No revelation, no grace. Stand, be still in your knowing and Rest. Praise and worship him. Only give God what he asks for. Give the man what he wants! We are workman together with God, not for God.
3. **Praise** – and watch God exhalt you. While you are yet in that place, the glory is passing. Even now, changing before your very eyes.

Whatever you do don't let the land possess you!

Kill It!
Duet. 9:1-6; 10:12-13; 11:10-31 *23, *13:1-9

Deut 9:1-7

Hear, O Israel: Thou art to pass over Jordan this day,(starting today, position your self) to go in to possess nations greater and mightier than thyself, cities great and fenced up to heaven,

2 A people great and tall, the children of the Anakims, whom thou knowest, and of whom thou hast heard say, Who can stand before the children of Anak!

3 Understand therefore this day, that the LORD thy God is he which goeth over before thee; as a consuming fire he shall destroy them, and he shall bring them down before thy face: so shalt thou drive them out, and destroy them quickly, as the LORD hath said unto thee. The Lord thy God is a consuming fire that goes before you to drive your enemies out. The battle is the Lord's!

4 Speak not thou in thine heart, after that the LORD thy God hath cast them out from before thee, saying, For my righteousness the LORD hath brought me in to possess this land: but for the wickedness of these nations the LORD doth drive them out from before thee. It's not that you have been so good, but they have been so bad.

5 Not for thy righteousness, or for the uprightness of thine heart, dost thou go to possess their land: but for the wickedness of these nations the LORD thy God doth drive them out from before thee, and that he may perform the word which the LORD sware unto thy fathers, Abraham, Isaac, and Jacob. God has to keep His word. It's all for His name sake

6 Understand therefore, that the LORD thy God giveth thee not this good land to possess it for thy righteousness; for thou art a stiffnecked people.

Deut 12:2-3

2 Ye shall utterly destroy all the places, wherein the nations which ye shall possess served their gods, upon the high mountains, and upon the hills, and under every green tree: You can not conquer what you conform to. Conquer and not conform, destroy all.

3 And ye shall overthrow their altars, and break their pillars, and burn their groves with fire; and ye shall hew down the graven images of their gods, and destroy the names of them out of that place. Change, overthrow, let the only true and living God come forth.

Deut 12:32 What thing soever I command you, observe to do it: thou shalt not add thereto, nor diminish from it. Completely Obey! No Compromising!

Deut 13:1-9

If there arise among you a prophet, or a dreamer of dreams, and giveth thee a sign or a wonder,

2 And the sign or the wonder come to pass, whereof he spake unto thee, saying, Let us go after other gods, which thou hast not known, and let us serve them;

3 Thou shalt not hearken unto the words of that prophet, or that dreamer of dreams: for the LORD your God proveth you, to know whether ye love the LORD your God with all your heart and with all your soul.

4 Ye shall walk after the LORD your God, and fear him, and keep his commandments, and obey his voice, and ye shall serve him, and cleave unto him.

5 And that prophet, or that dreamer of dreams, shall be put to death; Kill It! because he hath spoken to turn you away from the LORD your God, which brought you out of the land of Egypt, and redeemed you out of the house of bondage, to thrust thee out of the way which the LORD thy

God commanded thee to walk in. So shalt thou put the evil away from the midst of thee.

6 If thy brother, the son of thy mother, or thy son, or thy daughter, or the wife of thy bosom, or thy friend, which is as thine own soul, entice thee secretly, saying, Let us go and serve other gods, which thou hast not known, thou, nor thy fathers;

7 Namely, of the gods of the people which are round about you, nigh unto thee, or far off from thee, from the one end of the earth even unto the other end of the earth;

8 Thou shalt not consent unto him, nor hearken unto him; neither shall thine eye pity him, neither shalt thou spare, neither shalt thou conceal him:

9 But thou shalt surely kill him; thine hand shall be first upon him to put him to death, and afterwards the hand of all the people. Kill It! Not the man but the spirit, whatever it may be. Anything and anyone who draws you away from the plan of God. You must stand fast and don't let the enemy use those of influence to move you. You must stay close to God in your relationship to know when he has shifted. Not all will understand the way God is leading you. No one can lead you where they have not dared to go themselves. Sometimes what others don't understand and have not experienced, they will reject. But this does not mean that God has not spoken it to you. **Phil 1:16-20** The one preach Christ of contention, not sincerely, supposing to add affliction to my bonds: Does not have a clue what God is doing for God has not revealed it to them.

17 But the other of love, **knowing,** (has been there and done that), that I am **set** for the defence of the gospel. That God may defend me and be glorified!

18 What then? notwithstanding, every way, whether in pretence, or in truth, Christ is preached; and I therein do rejoice, yea, and will rejoice.

19 For **I know,** (you are the only one who has to know), that this shall turn to my salvation through your prayer, and the supply of the Spirit of Jesus Christ,

20 According to my earnest expectation and my hope, that in nothing I shall be ashamed, but that with **all boldness**, (This is the only way to be when going against all odds), as always, so now also Christ shall be magnified in my body, whether it be by life, or by death. Some have gotten so caught up in sin that they have become reprobate and can not see the things of God because the eye is evil and in darkness.

Jude 8-10 Likewise also these filthy dreamers defile the flesh, despise dominion, is not this what God commanded in the beginning? and speak evil of dignities.

9 Yet Michael the archangel, when contending with the devil he disputed about the body of Moses, durst not bring against him a railing accusation, but said, The Lord rebuke thee.

10 But these speak evil of those things which they know not: without understanding but what they know naturally, as brute beasts, in those things they corrupt themselves. But you are not the first. Look at Abraham, Noah and Jesus. He came to his own and they knew him not. **John 1:10-11** He was in the world, and the world was made by him, and the world knew him not. 11 He came unto his own, and his own received him not. So think it not strange, you're not the first.

Hindrances to Possessing the Land

1. Pride - Deut 9:4-6

4 Speak not thou in thine heart, after that the LORD thy God hath cast them out from before thee, saying, For my righteousness the LORD hath brought me in to possess this land: but for the wickedness of these nations the LORD doth drive them out from before thee.

5 Not for thy righteousness, or for the uprightness of thine heart, dost thou go to possess their land: but for the wickedness of these nations the LORD thy God doth drive them out from before thee, and that he may perform the word which the LORD sware unto thy fathers, Abraham, Isaac, and Jacob.

6 Understand therefore, that the LORD thy God giveth thee not this good land to possess it for thy righteousness; for thou art a stiffnecked people. It's not about you, But that God might be glorified! Grace is given for his purpose. For his names sake. **Isa 43:25** I, even I, am he that blotteth out thy transgressions for mine own sake, and will not remember thy sins.

2. Fear - Deut 11:23-28 Then will the LORD drive out all these nations from before you, and ye shall possess greater nations and mightier than yourselves.

24 Every place whereon the soles of your feet shall tread shall be yours: from the wilderness and Lebanon, from the river, the river Euphrates, even unto the uttermost sea shall your coast be.

25 There shall no man be able to stand before you: for the LORD your God shall lay the fear of you and the dread of you upon all the land that ye shall tread upon, as he hath said unto you.

26 Behold, I set before you this day a blessing and a curse;

27 A blessing, if ye obey the commandments of the LORD your God, which I command you this day:

28 And a curse, if ye will not obey the commandments of the LORD your God, but turn aside out of the way which I command you this day, to go after other gods, which ye have not known. Fear brings about disobedience. Just do it! You must trust God at his word.

3. Self-righteousness - Deut 12:8-9 Ye shall not do after all the things that we do here this day, every man whatsoever is right in his own eyes.

9 For ye are not as yet come to the rest and to the inheritance, which the LORD your God giveth you. You have not arrived! God didn't ask for your opinion.

Prov 16:25 There is a way that seemeth right unto a man, but the end thereof are the ways of death.

Rom 12:3 For I say, through the grace given unto me, to every man that is among you, not to think of himself more highly than he ought to think; but to think soberly, according as God hath dealt to every man the measure of faith. Don't fool yourself, your are not there yet.

4. Lust, Idolatry - Deut 11:16-17 Take heed to yourselves, that your heart be not deceived, and ye turn aside, and serve other gods, and worship them;

17 And then the LORD's wrath be kindled against you, and he shut up the heaven, that there be no rain, and that the land yield not her fruit; and lest ye perish quickly from off the good land which the LORD giveth you

18 Therefore shall ye lay up these my words in your heart and in your soul, and bind them for a sign upon your hand, that they may be as frontlets between your eyes. No other gods.

5. Rebellion - Deut 11:28 And a curse, if ye will not obey the commandments of the LORD your God, but turn aside out of the way which I command you this day, to go after other gods, which ye have not known.

Deut 12:32 What thing soever I command you, observe to do it: thou shalt not add thereto, nor diminish from it. Blessing if ye obey and curse if ye rebel. Your land is wherever you stand, matters of the heart. Even in prison God gave Joseph favor. Although the coat represents being clothed in righteousness, the blessing is not in the coat, but in the relationship or covenant of the heart. **The key to possessing is Obedience. Believing and trusting, positions you to walk in dominion!**

Kill It II
A Desert Baby Genocide
Joshua 5:2-9

Gal 5:19-21

Now the works of the flesh are manifest, which are these; Adultery, fornication, uncleanness, lasciviousness,

20 Idolatry, witchcraft, hatred, variance, emulations, wrath, strife, seditions, heresies,

21 Envyings, murders, drunkenness, revellings, and such like: of the which I tell you before, as I have also told you in time past, that they which do such things shall not inherit the kingdom of God.

Josh 5:2-6

At that time the LORD said unto Joshua, Make thee sharp knives, and circumcise again the children of Israel the second time.

3 And Joshua made him sharp knives, and circumcised the children of Israel at the hill of the foreskins. Obedience

4 And this is the cause why Joshua did circumcise: All the people that came out of Egypt, that were males, even all the men of war, died in the wilderness by the way, after they came out of Egypt.

5 Now all the people that came out were circumcised: but all the people that were born in the wilderness by the way as they came forth out of Egypt, them they had not circumcised.

6 For the children of Israel walked forty years in the wilderness, till all the people that were men of war, which came out of Egypt, were consumed, because they obeyed not the voice of the LORD: unto whom the LORD sware that he would not shew them the land, which the LORD sware

unto their fathers that he would give us, a land that floweth with milk and honey.

These were those that were chosen to help lead the people, not just limited to male. All were consumed. Leadership must first be circumcised. For whatever is found in the body reflects leadership. These men of war should have made it, but why not? It is not enough to be equipped for the battle, if we're not going to OBEY our Commanding Chief! Being arrogant, cocky, prideful, self-righteous, murmuring and complaining, and questioning God are matters of the heart and must be circumcised. **Deut 30:6** And the LORD thy God will circumcise thine heart, and the heart of thy seed, to love the LORD thy God with all thine heart, and with all thy soul, that thou mayest live. God must have complete obedience, don't add nor take away! **Deut 12:32** What thing soever I command you, observe to do it: thou shalt not add thereto, nor diminish from it.

Joshua 5:7-9

7 And their children, whom he raised up in their stead, them Joshua circumcised: for they were uncircumcised, because they had not circumcised them by the way. Although the first generation had been circumcised, it represented the old covenant which was based on works of the flesh. This circumcision was also symbolic, representing a new and better way that was still yet to come through a new generation, but some things must first die away. These children were not circumcised because their parents failed to teach them as they were commanded. **Deut 11:18-20** Therefore shall ye lay up these my words in your heart and in your soul, and bind them for a sign upon your hand, that they may be as frontlets between your eyes.

19 And ye shall teach them your children, speaking of them when thou sittest in thine house, and when thou walkest by the way, when thou liest down, and when thou risest up.

20 And thou shalt write them upon the door posts of thine house, and upon thy gates: because they murmured and complained, worshipped idol gods and did all manner of evil, their children were exposed to this ungrateful spirit, and their hearts were uncircumcised. If we being circumcised, turn

our backs on God and go back to a lifestyle of the world (representing Egypt mentality), and fail to pass on Godly morals, by training up our children in the fear and admonition of the Lord, then that generation will have to be circumcised again. This renews covenant.

8 And it came to pass, when they had done circumcising all the people, that they abode in their places in the camp, till they were whole.

9 And the LORD said unto Joshua, This day have I rolled away the reproach of Egypt from off you. Wherefore the name of the place is called Gilgal unto this day. When the heart is truly circumcised, God cuts away the desires of Egypt, by renewing the mind. **Heb 11:15-16** And truly, if they had been mindful of that country from whence they came out, they might have had opportunity to have returned.

16 But now they desire a better country, that is, an heavenly: wherefore God is not ashamed to be called their God: for he hath prepared for them a city.

John 14:30 Hereafter I will not talk much with you: for the prince of this world cometh, and hath nothing in me. Nothing can be found in you.

Being a chosen generation for such a time as this, we all have had to go through a wilderness experience. In this place some things died in us and some things were born. Not all that died, needed to die; some things we let slip by losing focus, and not all that was born needed to be born; some things we came out with due to the extremity of the persecution or the process. What should have made us better, made us bitter and because God has a set time, we came out but now must deal with some things before we can go in.

Now we can enter into that place of Rest promised.

Deut 11:10-12

10 For the land, whither thou goest in to possess it, is **not as** the land of Egypt, from whence ye came out, where thou sowedst thy seed, and wateredst it with thy foot, as a garden of herbs: Again Egypt represents the

works of flesh. In Egypt you were responsible for making things happen. It was all based on your works.

11 But the land, whither ye go to possess it, is a land of hills and valleys, and drinketh water of the rain of heaven: Hills are what we all want to experience, for they represent the good of times and prosperity. But in God's plan, the path of righteousness, there are also valleys. Valleys are there to prepare us for the next mountain. When God gets ready to take us to a higher mountain, he must first bring us down and take us through a valley to prepare our spirit to receive the blessing. We want from faith to faith and from glory to glory, but we must understand that the mountain is not the glory. The glory is in the valley. The mountain is the provision. The glory is how you respond while in the valley. Your faithfulness, failing to draw back; your character, failing to compromise, That's Glory!

Ps 23:1-6

The LORD is my shepherd; I shall not want.

2 He maketh me to lie down in green pastures: he leadeth me beside the still waters.

3 He restoreth my soul: he leadeth me in the paths of righteousness for his name's sake. These are the hill experiences.

4 Yea, though I walk through the valley of the shadow of death, I will fear no evil: for thou art with me; thy rod and thy staff they comfort me. Here is where the glory is. It is where his strength is made perfect in our weakness.

2 Cor 12:9 And he said unto me, My grace is sufficient for thee: for my strength is made perfect in weakness. Most gladly therefore will I rather glory in my infirmities, that the power of Christ may rest upon me.

Where he shows **Eph 1:19,** what is the exceeding greatness of his power to usward who believe, according to the working of his mighty power, we must pass the glory test, then comes the provision, the manifested promise.

5 Thou preparest a table before me in the presence of mine enemies: thou anointest my head with oil; my cup runneth over.

6 Surely goodness and mercy shall follow me all the days of my life: and I will dwell in the house of the LORD for ever. The mountain, his presence.

Duet. 11:12

12 A land which the LORD thy **God careth for**: the eyes of the LORD thy God are always upon it, from the beginning of the year even unto the end of the year. A PLACE OF REST! It is obtained through faith and patience. Through the act of OBEDIENCE. FOR ALL THINGS ARE READY!

Matt 22:4 Again, he sent forth other servants, saying, Tell them which are bidden, Behold, I have prepared my dinner: my oxen and my fatlings are killed, and all things are ready: come unto the marriage. **Heb 4:3** For we which have believed do enter into rest, as he said, As I have sworn in my wrath, if they shall enter into my rest: **although the works were finished from the foundation of the world.**

Duet 12: 2-3,9

2 Ye shall utterly destroy all the places, wherein the nations which ye shall possess served their gods, upon the high mountains, and upon the hills, and under every green tree:

3 And ye shall overthrow their altars, and break their pillars, and burn their groves with fire; and ye shall hew down the graven images of their gods, and destroy the names of them out of that place.

9 For ye are not as yet come to the rest and to the inheritance, which the LORD your God giveth you. In order to possess the land we must overthrow other gods and their kingdoms and not conform to them. We can't change what we conform to. This is the need for circumcision. That they may enter that place of Rest. Believing establishes victory. **2 Chron 20:20** And they rose early in the morning, and went forth into the wilderness of Tekoa: and as they went forth, Jehoshaphat stood and said, Hear me, O Judah, and ye inhabitants of Jerusalem; Believe in the

LORD your God, so shall ye be established; believe his prophets, so shall ye prosper. Our land is first established in our hearts. We can't partake of our inheritance until we first come into REST.

Because God's fighting for us. **2 Chron 20:15** And he said, Hearken ye, all Judah, and ye inhabitants of Jerusalem, and thou king Jehoshaphat, Thus saith the LORD unto you, Be not afraid nor dismayed by reason of this great multitude; for the battle is not yours, but God's.

Deut 9:3 Understand therefore this day, that the LORD thy God is he which goeth over before thee; as a consuming fire he shall destroy them, and he shall bring them down before thy face: so shalt thou drive them out, and destroy them quickly, as the LORD hath said unto thee

To maintain our inheritance, REST must become a lifestyle once we enter.

Deut 11:10-12 For the land, whither thou goest in to possess it, is not as the land of Egypt, from whence ye came out, where thou sowedst thy seed, and wateredst it with thy foot, as a garden of herbs: What worked in Egypt won't work! What God promised can not be birthed through the flesh, nor can it be maintained through natural means. IT IS THE POINT OF NO RETURN!

11 But the land, whither ye go to possess it, is a land of hills and valleys, and drinketh water of the rain of heaven:

12 A land which the LORD thy God careth for: the eyes of the LORD thy God are always upon it, from the beginning of the year even unto the end of the year.

Deut 8:2-3

2 And thou shalt remember all the way which the LORD thy God led thee these forty years in the wilderness, to humble thee, and to prove thee, to know what was in thine heart, whether thou wouldest keep his commandments, or no.

3 And he humbled thee, and suffered thee to hunger, and fed thee with manna, which thou knewest not, neither did thy fathers know; that he might make thee know that man doth not live by bread only, but by every word that proceedeth out of the mouth of the LORD doth man live.

The wilderness was a place of preparation to prepare the heart. A place of trying and purifying that we might know what's in our hearts because God already knows. A place where our hearts become surrendered to him. It's really where we fall in love with Him. It is the place where we enter into covenant, become a sacrifice on the altar of sacrifice, see ourselves in his word that we might be cleanse at the Brazen Lavar. The place where we enter into the Holy Place and receive the eyes of our understanding opened by revelation given at the Lamp Stand, being strengthened in our inner man by eating of his word, at the Table of Shewbread and learn to offer up a sweet smelling savor of pure worship at the Table of Incense. That we learn to walk in the Spirit, abiding in the presence of God in the Most Holy Place.

When Abram stepped out in faith to leave his country, he stepped into a whole new way of life and never went back to the old way of living. He possessed a new way of thinking. **Luke 9:62** And Jesus said unto him, No man, having put his hand to the plough, and looking back, is fit for the kingdom of God. But from faith to faith and to glory to glory, God always keeps his word.

Choose Ye This Day!

Phil. 3:12-14; forgetting the past and pressing toward the future

Heb 10:5-17 take away the old and establish the new

Joshua 24:12-15

11 And ye went over Jordan, and came unto Jericho: and the men of Jericho fought against you, the Amorites, and the Perizzites, and the Canaanites, and the Hittites, and the Girgashites, the Hivites, and the Jebusites; and I delivered them into your hand.

12 And I sent the hornet before you, which drave them out from before you, even the two kings of the Amorites; but not with thy sword, nor with thy bow.

13 And I have given you a land for which ye did not labour, and cities which ye built not, and ye dwell in them; of the vineyards and oliveyards which ye planted not do ye eat.

14 Now therefore fear the LORD, and serve him in sincerity and in truth: and put away the gods which your fathers served on the other side of the flood, and in Egypt; and serve ye the LORD.

15 And if it seem evil unto you to serve the LORD, choose you this day whom ye will serve; whether the gods which your fathers served that were on the other side of the flood, or the gods of the Amorites, in whose land ye dwell: but as for me and my house, we will serve the LORD. For he shall have no other God before him. Can't serve both. **Luke 16:13** servant can serve two masters: for either he will hate the one, and love the other; or else he will hold to the one, and despise the other. Ye cannot serve God and mammon.

Rom 6:16 Know ye not, that to whom ye yield yourselves servants to obey, his servants ye are to whom ye obey; whether of sin unto death, or of obedience unto righteousness? Choosing always entails looking at the past, the present and the future to compare options. But when God's orders us to choose, he also eliminates options. Because the truth of the matter is, **John 15:16** Ye have not chosen me, but I have chosen you, and ordained you, that ye should go and bring forth fruit, and that your fruit should remain: that whatsoever ye shall ask of the Father in my name, he may give it you. And in His choosing, he has great plans. **Jer 29:11** For I know the thoughts that I think toward you, saith the LORD, thoughts of peace, and not of evil, to give you an expected end. His plans require us to forget what use to be and even what is and strive for a new and better way.

Phil 3:12-14

12 Not as though I had already attained, either were already perfect: but I follow after, if that I may apprehend that for which also I am apprehended of Christ Jesus. Paul says not as though I have already become what he has called me to be, but I continue to pursue or follow after that I may lay hold to, become or capture that for which I am also captured or chosen to do and become. What are you following after, in hot pursuit of?

13 Brethren, I count not myself to have apprehended: but this one thing I do, forgetting those things which are behind, and reaching forth unto those things which are before, I don't claim to have captured or completely stepped into, but this one step forget, press and reach. We can't press and reach forth without first forgetting. Like the Father, Son and the Holy Ghost, they are all one. Paul made a conscience decision that he was not looking back. We know what's behind and where that road leads, so it's time to try something different. This decision forces us to:

**cancel past options
**arouses curiosity, creating a hunger and thirst for righteousness
**produces expectancy to give birth to change

14 I press toward the mark for the prize of the high calling of God in Christ Jesus. In order to reach this mark or place where God is calling us, we must come up higher in the things of God. Then we can receive the prize or promise.

Until we forget the past, we will never hunger for what's ahead.

Heb 11:15

15 And truly, if they had been mindful of that country from whence they came out, they might have had opportunity to have returned. Forgetting and remembering is a battle of the mind.

Heb 10:5-17

The old and the new:

5 Wherefore when he cometh into the world, he saith, Sacrifice and offering thou wouldest not, but a body hast thou prepared me:

6 In burnt offerings and sacrifices for sin thou hast had no pleasure.

7 Then said I, Lo, I come (in the volume of the book it is written of me,) to do thy will, O God.

8 Above when he said, Sacrifice and offering and burnt offerings and offering for sin thou wouldest not, neither hadst pleasure therein; which are offered by the law;

9 Then said he, Lo, I come to do thy will, O God. He taketh away the first, that he may establish the second.

10 By the which will we are sanctified through the offering of the body of Jesus Christ once for all.

11 And every priest standeth daily ministering and offering oftentimes the same sacrifices, which can never take away sins:

12 But this man, after he had offered one sacrifice for sins for ever, sat down on the right hand of God;

13 From henceforth expecting till his enemies be made his footstool.

14 For by one offering he hath perfected for ever them that are sanctified.

15 Whereof the Holy Ghost also is a witness to us: for after that he had said before,

16 This is the covenant that I will make with them after those days, saith the Lord, I will put my laws into their hearts, and in their minds will I write them;

17 And their sins and iniquities will I remember no more.

What worked then, won't work now. It wasn't perfect then, but God allowed it, and knew that he had a better plan. This plan was designed to establish a pattern of belief, laying a foundation of faith. It was just the beginning of faith. And even though God already knew it would not accomplish his ultimate goal, it was his will for that time. It was a pattern of what was to come, it was not the real deal.

Heb 8:5-8 Who serve unto the example and shadow of heavenly things, as Moses was admonished of God when he was about to make the tabernacle: for, See, saith he, that thou make all things according to the pattern shewed to thee in the mount.

6 But now hath he obtained a more excellent ministry, by how much also he is the mediator of a better covenant, which was established upon better promises.

7 For if that first covenant had been faultless, then should no place have been sought for the second.

8 For finding fault with them, he saith, Behold, the days come, saith the Lord, when I will make a new covenant with the house of Israel and with the house of Judah:

Heb 9:8-14

8 The Holy Ghost this signifying, that the way into the holiest of all was not yet made manifest, while as the first tabernacle was yet standing:

9 Which was a figure for the time then present, in which were offered both gifts and sacrifices, that could not make him that did the service perfect, as pertaining to the conscience;

10 Which stood only in meats and drinks, and divers washings, and carnal ordinances, imposed on them until the time of reformation.

11 But Christ being come an high priest of good things to come, by a greater and more perfect tabernacle, not made with hands, that is to say, not of this building;

12 Neither by the blood of goats and calves, but by his own blood he entered in once into the holy place, having obtained eternal redemption for us.

13 For if the blood of bulls and of goats, and the ashes of an heifer sprinkling the unclean, sanctifieth to the purifying of the flesh:

14 How much more shall the blood of Christ, who through the eternal Spirit offered himself without spot to God, purge your conscience from dead works to serve the living God? That was then, this is now!

Heb 9:23

It was therefore necessary that the patterns of things in the heavens should be purified with these; but the heavenly things themselves with better sacrifices than these. Even in life today, it is necessary that some things happen. It was necessary that some things ended, it set things in motion for the better way.

Heb 10:8-9

Above when he said, Sacrifice and offering and burnt offerings and offering for sin thou wouldest not, neither hadst pleasure therein; which are offered by the law;

9 Then said he, Lo, I come to do thy will, O God. He taketh away the first, that he may establish the second. What God accepted then, he wants no part of now. Yes, he allowed it but now he's moving it to establish a better way. What is it in your life that you are trying to hold on to that God is through with! Is it a job, a relationship, a position in church or is a career. What have you allowed in this season of your life, that God says has ended. If the five wise virgins had tried to hold on to the foolish virgins, they would have missed their chance for promotion even though they were ready. Whatever it is, let it go! God has so much more and it's better.

Heb 10:11-20

11 And every priest standeth daily ministering and offering oftentimes the same sacrifices, which can never take away sins:

12 But this man, after he had offered **one** sacrifice for sins for ever, sat down on the right hand of God;

13 From henceforth expecting till his enemies be made his footstool.

14 For by one offering he hath perfected for ever them that are sanctified.

15 Whereof the Holy Ghost also is a witness to us: for after that he had said before,

16 This is the covenant that I will make with them after those days, saith the Lord, I will put my laws into their hearts, and in their minds will I write them;

17 And their sins and iniquities will I remember no more.

18 Now where remission of these is, there is no more offering for sin.

19 Having therefore, brethren, boldness to enter into the holiest by the blood of Jesus,

20 By a new and living way, which he hath consecrated for us, through the veil, that is to say, his flesh;

Jesus took the work out of the equation. He finished the work for us. Although we still have to live a life pleasing to him and put him first in all things. And when we miss the mark, we simply repent and believe that what he says is true. Catch this! All that you did before you came to Christ or before you repented God says, "I forgot, I don't remember". God says, "I'm reaching and pressing, where are you"?

Even after Abram had sinned and bore a son with Hagar, God did not bring up his failure, but just simply reminded him that the promise was still good. **Gen 17:1-5** And when Abram was ninety years old and nine, the LORD appeared to Abram, and

2 And I will make my covenant between me and thee, and will multiply thee exceedingly.

3 And Abram fell on his face: and God talked with him, saying,

4 As for me, behold, my covenant is with thee, and thou shalt be a father of many nations.

5 Neither shall thy name any more be called Abram, but thy name shall be Abraham; for a father of many nations have I made thee. When we partake of covenant, there is a name change. Just like in a marriage. And not only is the name changed, strength is exchanged for weakness. **2 Cor 12:5-9** Of such an one will I glory: yet of myself I will not glory, but in mine infirmities.

6 For though I would desire to glory, I shall not be a fool; for I will say the truth: but now I forbear, lest any man should think of me above that which he seeth me to be, or that he heareth of me.

7 And lest I should be exalted above measure through the abundance of the revelations, there was given to me a thorn in the flesh, the messenger of Satan to buffet me, lest I should be exalted above measure.

8 For this thing I besought the Lord thrice, that it might depart from me.

9 And he said unto me, My grace is sufficient for thee: **for my strength is made perfect in weakness.** Most gladly therefore will I rather glory in my infirmities, that the power of Christ may rest upon me.

Heb 4:16 Let us therefore come boldly unto the throne of grace, that we may obtain mercy, and find grace to help in time of need. We must come with a clear conscience, knowing that we have been redeemed and cleansed.

1 John 3:19-22

19 And hereby we know that we are of the **truth,** (his word) and shall assure our hearts before him.

20 For if our heart condemn us, God is greater than our heart, and knoweth all things. If we are in condemnation, then we are not in faith, coming boldly. But yet we are still carrying the concern or issue, and he can not be touched, (can't touch the helm of his garment) with that infirmity. Jesus has already carried it and won't carry it again. So we must first get in the place of confidence in his word, then come boldly.

21 Beloved, if our heart condemn us not, then have we **confidence** toward God.

22 And whatsoever we ask, we receive of him, because we keep his commandments, and do those things that are pleasing in his sight. Because we are in truth and ask with confidence, we know. **1 John 5:14-15**

And this is the confidence that we have in him, that, if we ask any thing according to his will, he heareth us:

15 And if we know that he hear us, whatsoever we ask, we know that we have the petitions that we desired of him.

Faith is the substance of things hoped for, but confidence is the evidence of your knowing!

How to Hold on to Your Dreams
Hebrews 10:35-36; 11:1

Heb 10:35-36

Cast not away therefore your confidence, which hath great recompence of reward.

36 For ye have need of patience, that, after ye have done the will of God, ye might receive the promise.

I 35 We must be confident in our dream.

A) Realize that the dream came from God and that He is the author and finisher.

Phil 2:13 For it is God which worketh in you both to will and to do of his good pleasure.

Phil 1:6 Being confident of this very thing, that he which hath begun a good work in you will perform it until the day of Jesus Christ:

B) Except he build the house, they that build, build in vain. (Ps. **127:1**)

Matt 6:33 But seek ye first the kingdom of God, and his righteousness; and all these things shall be added unto you.

Prov 3:5-6 Trust in the LORD with all thine heart; and lean not unto thine own understanding.

6 In all thy ways acknowledge him, and he shall direct thy paths.

We must die to our will and way of fulfilling our dream and seek God's way. After he has given direction or instructions, we must do just that and wait for the dream to overtake us, while seeking Him. Our dream is hidden in Him.

Gal 2:20-21 I am crucified with Christ: nevertheless I live; yet not I, but Christ liveth in me: and the life which I now live in the flesh I live by the faith of the Son of God, who loved me, and gave himself for me.

21 I do not frustrate the grace of God: for if righteousness come by the law, then Christ is dead in vain.

Matt 10:38-39 And he that taketh not his cross, and followeth after me, is not worthy of me.

39 He that findeth his life shall lose it: and he that loseth his life for my sake shall find it.

Deut 28:1-2 And it shall come to pass, if thou shalt hearken diligently unto the voice of the LORD thy God, to observe and to do all his commandments which I command thee this day, that the LORD thy God will set thee on high above all nations of the earth:

2 And all these blessings shall come on thee, and overtake thee, if thou shalt hearken unto the voice of the LORD thy God.

II 36 We must allow God to build character in us while we wait for his manifestation.

A) We must possess patience, which enables us to endure and enjoy the dream. Patience is the ability to bear long waiting, or anything unpleasant, calm and without complaining.

Patience to receive a complete and finished work of God.

James 1:4 But let patience have her perfect work, that ye may be perfect and entire, wanting nothing. Nothing lacking and nothing broken, the

Endurance, the strength to finish, the ability to last.

Matt 24:13 But he that shall endure unto the end, the same shall be saved.

Matt 10:22 And ye shall be hated of all men for my name's sake: but he that endureth to the end shall be saved.

Ps 138:8 The LORD will perfect that which concerneth me: thy mercy, O LORD, endureth for ever: forsake not the works of thine own hands.

God completes through His enduring mercy. He gives mercy until completion. He had already deposited and knows exactly how much is needed to finish what he starts.

III 37 The dream has a set, appointed time and will surely come.

Hab 2:3 For the vision is yet for an appointed time, but at the end it shall speak, and not lie: though it tarry, wait for it; because it will surely come, it will not tarry.

Gal 6:9 And let us not be weary in well doing: for in due season we shall reap, if we faint not.

Due season always comes. When we forsake all for Christ, he always pays on time. We are His workmanship. **Eph 2:10** For we are his workmanship, created in Christ Jesus unto good works, which God hath before ordained that we should walk in them. Chosen, and quitting is not an option!

IV Patience and Endurance are signs of trust which is equal to faith, but can only manifest through the word. (prayer, faith and praise)

Prayer "The Word"

Prayer is the birthing place where the womb of the spirit releases, PUSH!

Phil 4:6 Be careful for nothing; but in every thing by prayer and supplication with thanksgiving let your requests be made known unto God.

Your request, the word, is the baby that you are pregnant with.

Prayer is the battle ground, where warfare takes place, where victory is secured (in the mind). **Phil 4:7** And the peace of God, which passeth all understanding, shall keep your hearts and minds through Christ Jesus.

Prayer is the court room where we plead our cause. God the Father is judge, Jesus is our advocate, lawyer and the Holy Spirit is the jury. **Ps 35:1** Plead my cause, O LORD, with them that strive with me: fight against them that fight against me.

B) Faith The Word"

Heb 11:1 Now faith is the substance of things hoped for, the evidence of things not seen.

Substance, the material that can be seen or felt.

Evidence, the information that proves a statement, supports a belief or makes a matter more clear. **John 1:1-3** In the beginning was the Word, and the Word was with God, and the Word was God.

2 The same was in the beginning with God.

3 All things were made by him; and without him was not any thing made that was made.

Evidence assures us, a guarantee, **Isa 55:11** So shall my word be that goeth forth out of my mouth: it shall not return unto me void, but it shall accomplish that which I please, and it shall prosper in the thing whereto I sent it.

Evidence is already done, finished. Matt 22:4 Again, he sent forth other servants, saying, Tell them which are bidden, Behold, I have prepared my dinner: my oxen and my fatlings are killed, and all things are ready: come unto the marriage.

Heb 4:3 For we which have believed do enter into rest, as he said, As I have sworn in my wrath, if they shall enter into my rest: although the works were finished from the foundation of the world.

Ps 119:89 For ever, O LORD, thy word is settled in heaven.

1 Peter 1:4 To an inheritance incorruptible, and undefiled, and that fadeth not away, reserved in heaven for you, **Decrees and establishes, 1 John 5:14-15** And this is the confidence that we have in him, that, if we ask any thing according to his will, he heareth us:

15 And if we know that he hear us, whatsoever we ask, we know that we have the petitions that we desired of him.

Eph 3:11-12 According to the eternal purpose which he purposed in Christ Jesus our Lord:

12 In whom we have boldness and access with confidence by the faith of him.

C) Praise initiates the victory!

Isa 42:12-14 Let them give glory unto the LORD, and declare his praise in the islands.

13 The LORD shall go forth as a mighty man, he shall stir up jealousy like a man of war: he shall cry, yea, roar; he shall prevail against his enemies.

14 I have long time holden my peace; I have been still, and refrained myself: now will I cry like a travailing woman; I will destroy and devour at once.

Praise gives access. Rom 5:2 By whom also we have access by faith into this grace wherein we stand, and rejoice in hope of the glory of God.

V 38 Don't Give Up, Don't Quit!

We can't drawback (quit, stop or turn around) we must continue to pursue.

A) **Draw near to God. James 4:7-8** Submit yourselves therefore to God. Resist the devil, and he will flee from you.

8 Draw nigh to God, and he will draw nigh to you. Cleanse your hands, ye sinners; and purify your hearts, ye double minded.

Don't change your confession or profession. Heb 10:23 Let us hold fast the profession of our faith without wavering; (for he is faithful that promised;) Don't let the enemy force you to change your mind. Be like Jacob. Don't let go until God blesses you. He doesn't have a choice when it comes to his word.

1 Peter 5:8-9 Be sober, be vigilant; because your adversary the devil, as a roaring lion, walketh about, seeking whom he may devour:

9 Whom resist stedfast in the faith, knowing that the same afflictions are accomplished in your brethren that are in the world.

C) KEEP HOPE ALIVE! Rom 15:4 For whatsoever things were written aforetime were written for our learning, that we through patience and comfort of the scriptures might have hope.

Rom 8:24-25 For we are saved by hope: but hope that is seen is not hope: for what a man seeth, why doth he yet hope for?

25 But if we hope for that we see not, then do we with patience wait for it.

Rom 5:3-5 And not only so, but we glory in tribulations also: knowing that tribulation worketh patience;

4 And patience, experience; and experience, hope:

5 And hope maketh not ashamed; because the love of God is shed abroad in our hearts by the Holy Ghost which is given unto us. You will not be shamed!

Possessing Canaan!

Josh 3:1-5

3:1 And Joshua rose early in the morning; and they removed from Shittim, and came to Jordan, he and all the children of Israel, and lodged there before they passed over.

2 And it came to pass after three days, that the officers went through the host;

3 And they commanded the people, saying, When ye **see** the ark of the covenant of the LORD your God, and the priests the Levites bearing it, then ye shall remove from your place, and go after it. **1. You must have spiritual insight**; having ears that hear and eyes that can see when the

man of God is speaking a ramah word over your life. The word always goes before you and believing establishes you. **Num 10:33** And they departed from the mount of the LORD three days' journey: and the ark of the covenant of the LORD went before them in the three days' journey, to search out a resting place for them. **A) Whenever insight is given, God always requires a response. B) The faith call** To move from your place of comfort and go after it, pursue the word. **John 3:8** The wind bloweth where it listeth, and thou hearest the sound thereof, but canst not tell whence it cometh, and whither it goeth: so is every one that is born of the Spirit.

4 Yet there shall be a space (**time**) between you and it, about two thousand cubits by measure: come not near unto it, that ye may know the way by which ye must go: for ye have not passed this way heretofore. **2. Wait for God's timing! A) Instructions come after the call. B) To an unfamiliar path.** (A New Thing)

5 And Joshua said unto the people, Sanctify yourselves: for to morrow the LORD will do wonders among you. **3 FOCUS!**

A) **must produce an environment conducive for God to speak**. **Isa 30:15** For thus saith the Lord GOD, the Holy One of Israel; In returning and rest shall ye be saved; in quietness and in confidence shall be your strength: and ye would not.

B) **Deal with distractions. Ps 119:37** Turn away mine eyes from beholding vanity; and quicken thou me in thy way.

C) **Go before God with His word, speak the word only! Matt 10:20** For it is not ye that speak, but the Spirit of your Father which speaketh in you.

Instructions:
Josh 3:8-13

8 And thou shalt command the priests that bear the ark of the covenant, saying, When ye are come to the brink of the water of Jordan, ye shall stand still in Jordan. When positioned in your circumstance, now stand ye still.

Don't be double minded, tossed to and fro. Stand with the full armor and in confidence! Knowing that the battle is the Lord's.

9 And Joshua said unto the children of Israel, Come hither, and hear the words of the LORD your God.

10 And Joshua said, Hereby ye shall know that the living God is among you, and that he will without fail drive out from before you the Canaanites, and the Hittites, and the Hivites, and the Perizzites, and the Girgashites, and the Amorites, and the Jebusites.

11 Behold, the ark of the covenant of the Lord of all the earth passeth over before you into Jordan.

12 Now therefore take you twelve men out of the tribes of Israel, out of every tribe a man.

13 And it shall come to pass, as soon as the soles of the feet of the priests that bear the ark of the LORD, the Lord of all the earth, shall rest in the waters of Jordan, that the waters of Jordan shall be cut off from the waters that come down from above; and they shall stand upon an heap. Don't look at how big the situation is or how complicated it is God knows. It didn't matter how big the Jordan was all they had to do is come to the brink and put the sole of their feet in at the edge and the waters would open up. Just like the door does when you go to the grocery store. You are sure that it will open when you get to a certain place. You never wonder if it's going to get stuck or if it's even out of order, you walk up to that door fully pursuaded, confident that the door is operating properly and that you will get in. **Yea, God says just like that! Rest in the waters**, with peace, confidence and expectation. **No Fear!**

4. Obedience. Josh 3:14-17 And it came to pass, when the people removed from their tents, to pass over Jordan, and the priests bearing the ark of the covenant before the people;

15 And as they that bare the ark were come unto Jordan, and the feet of the priests that bare the ark were dipped in the brim of the water, (for Jordan overfloweth all his banks all the time of harvest,)

16 That the waters which came down from above stood and rose up upon an heap very far from the city Adam, that is beside Zaretan: and those that came down toward the sea of the plain, even the salt sea, failed, and were cut off: and the people passed over right against Jericho.

17 And the priests that bare the ark of the covenant of the LORD stood **firm** on dry ground in the midst of Jordan, and all the Israelites passed over on dry ground, until all the people were passed clean over Jordan. **Confidence is the evidence of your Knowing!**

The word comes before because it's harvest time. But without the seed of obedience, harvest can't manifest. **It's already done! So REST in the Jordan. As soon as you obey, there is a Sudden manifestation!**

5.) There is Grace to finish. Josh 4:10 For the priests which bare the ark stood in the midst of Jordan, until everything was finished that the LORD commanded Joshua to speak unto the people, according to all that Moses commanded Joshua: and the people hasted and passed over. **Many are called, but few are chosen. Anybody can start, but not everybody will finish.**

Wait for God to release you. Timing is everything! Josh 4:15-17 And the LORD spake unto Joshua, saying,

16 Command the priests that bear the ark of the testimony, that they come up out of Jordan.

17 Joshua therefore commanded the priests, saying, Come ye up out of Jordan. **The visionary has the authority from God to release the people. You must stay close to God to discern when It Is Finished!**

V

The Promotion

But as many as received him, to them gave he power to become the sons of God, even to them that believe on his name:
John 1:12

Elevation And Escalation

A HIGHER CALL TO WORSHIP, ANOTHER LEVEL OF PRAISE!
ISAIAH 55:6-13

Seek ye the LORD while he may be found, (**TIME AND SEASON)** call ye upon him while he is near: **SCHEDULE A VISITATION!**

7 Let the wicked forsake **his** way, (ACTIONS, SYSTEM, PRINCIPLES, STRATEGIES WAY OF DOING) and the unrighteous man his thoughts (MIND SET): and let him **return** unto the LORD, and he will have mercy upon him; and to our God, for he will abundantly pardon. (**RETURN TO THE KINGDOM OF GOD, HIS WAY OF DOING, HE IS WAITING TO RECEIVE YOU.)**

8 For my thoughts *are* not your thoughts, neither *are* your ways my ways, saith the LORD. (**THOUGHTS PRODUCE ACTIONS) ELEVATION**

9 For *as* the heavens are higher than the earth, so are my ways higher than your ways, and my thoughts than your thoughts. **THE MIND**

OF CHRIST IS MUCH HIGHER, WISER THAN THE MIND OF MAN, THEREFORE ARE HIS WAYS, STRATEGIES. WE MUST COME UP HIGHER, OUR THINKING IS TOO LOW! GOD HAS MORE, GREATER! BUT WE MUST CHANGE OUR THINKING!

PROV. 23:7 For as he thinketh in his heart, so *is* he: Eat and drink, saith he to thee; but his heart *is* not with thee. THE WORDS OF OUR MOUTH AND THE MEDITATIONS OF OUR HEART MUST AGREE.

ROM 10:10 For with the heart man believeth unto righteousness; and with the mouth confession is made unto salvation.

ONLY THE MIND OF GOD CAN PRODUCE THE WAYS OF GOD!

PROV. 14:12 There is a way which seemeth right unto a man, but the end thereof *are* the ways of death.

10 For as the rain cometh down, and the snow from heaven, and returneth not thither, but watereth the earth, and maketh it bring forth and bud, that it may give seed to the sower, and bread to the eater:

(IT HAS A PURPOSE. A STRATEGY TO PRODUCE PROVISION. A PROCESS)

11 **So shall my word be that goeth forth out of my mouth:(IT HAS A CYCLE THAT IT HAS TO COMPLETE. FIRST THE BLADE, THEN THE EAR THEN THE FULL CORN IN THE EAR)** it shall not return unto me void, but it shall accomplish that which I please, and it shall prosper *in the thing* whereto I sent it. **AS THE WORD GOETH FORTH OUT OF MY MOUTH, AS SOON AS, IT BEGINS IT'S PROCESS, IT BEGINS TO BE.**

ITS BECOMING!   IT'S SHIFTING!   IT'S AVENGING!

IT'S CHANGING!   IT'S CREATING!

HEB 4: 12 For the word of God *is* **quick, and powerful**, and sharper than any twoedged sword, **piercing** even to the **dividing asunder** of soul and spirit, and of the joints and marrow, and *is* a **discerner** of the thoughts and intents of the heart.

12 For ye shall go out with joy, and be led forth with peace: **THE WORK BEGINS IN ME FIRST** the mountains and the hills (**MIND BLOCKS STRONGHOLDS, FEAR ANXIETY, WORRY,**) shall beak forth before you into singing (**GARMENT OF PRAISE FOR THE SPIRIT OF HEAVINESS**), and all the trees (**MINDSETS, THOUGHT PATTERNS**) of the field shall clap *their* hands. (**ALL OUR THOUGHTS TURN TO PRAISE, WORSHIP AND HONOR**)

13 Instead of the **thorn (PAIN DEATH)** shall come up the fir tree, (, **LIFE**) and instead of the **brier** shall come up the myrtle tree: **WHEREVER THERE IS DEATH IT SHALL BE TURNED INTO LIFE**) and it shall be to the LORD for a name, (**AWESOME, MIGHTY, POWERFUL, OMNIPOTENT**), for an everlasting sign a (**A MEMORIAL**) *that* shall not be cut off. **WHAT GOD DOES, MAN CAN'T TAKE AWAY NOR ADD TO IT! WE MUST CONTINUE TO DECLARE THE WORD OF GOD AND TRUST IT TO RUN IT'S COURSE.**

PHIL 1:6 Being confident of this very thing, that he which hath begun a good work in you will **perform** *it* until the day of Jesus Christ: **THE PERFORMANCE IS THE PROCESS, STAGES AND PHASES.**

The Secret Place

PS 91:1-4; EX. 33:12-14;18-23

PS 91: 1-16 He that dwelleth in the secret place of the most High shall abide under the shadow of the Almighty.

2 I will say of the LORD, *He is* my refuge and my fortress: my God; in him will I trust.

3 Surely he shall deliver thee from the snare of the fowler, *and* from the noisome pestilence.

4 He shall cover thee with his feathers, and under his wings shalt thou trust: his truth *shall be thy* shield and buckler.

In the place of Divine Protection and Divined Intervention, we find peace, comfort even REST, in this Psalm. The Secret Place, the Place where God is , His Presence.

What exactly is the Secret Place and how do I dwell there that I might abide? How do I stay here in this place and still advance in my life?

**First, I must understand that this is not a physical place, but a place should be in the SPIRIT.

ISAIAH 55:8-9 For my thoughts *are* not your thoughts, neither *are* your ways my ways, saith the LORD.

9For *as* the heavens are higher than the earth, so are my ways higher than your ways, and my thoughts than your thoughts. THE LORD'S THOUGHTS ARE HIS WORDS. WE MUST ELEVATE OUR THINKING TO THE MIND, WAYS OF GOD, AGREE, UNITE WITH HIM TO BECOME LIKE HIM. THE GLORY OF GOD, THE KINGDOM OF GOD IS IN STAGES PHASES. THIS IS THE ONLY REASON FOR THE FACTS IS TO ALLOW US TO KNOW WHAT STAGE WE ARE IN, DURING THE PROCESS. FACTS ARE UPDATED EVERY MINUTE. TEMPORAL, AND WHAT WE CAN NOT SEE IS WORKING FOR US A FAR EXCEEDING WEIGHT IN GLORY!

2 CORN 4:17-18 For our light affliction, which is but for a moment, worketh for us a far more exceeding *and* eternal weight of glory;

18While we look not at the things which are seen, but at the things which are not seen: for the things which are seen *are* temporal; but the things which are not seen *are* eternal.

The SECRET PLACE IS A PLACE OF REST, WHERE WE CEASE FROM OUR OWN WORKS AND TRUST THE HAND OF GOD.

THE PLACE WHERE, NOT I, BUT THE FATHER IN ME THAT DOETH THE WORK.

JOHN 14:10 Believest thou not that I am in the Father, and the Father in me? the words that I speak unto you I speak not of myself: but the Father that dwelleth in me, he doeth the works.

MOSES AFTER HE HAD GOTTEN IN TROUBLE FOR SMITING THE ROCK WHEN TOLD TO SPEAK TO THE ROCK, QUESTIONS THE LORD ABOUT WHO WILL GO WITH HIM AND TO SHOW HIM HIS WAYS, THAT HE MIGHT KNOW HIM. THAT IS WHAT HE WAS TRYING TO DO WHEN INSTRUCTING MOSES TO SPEAK TO THE ROCK. THE LORD WAS TRYING TO GET MOSES TO SEE THE SYSTEM IN WHICH HE WAS OPERATING IN. THE CHILDREN OF ISRAEL HAD TO WORK WHEN IN EGYPT, BUT CANAAN WAS A PLACE OF REST, COMPLETE OBEDIENCE TO THE VOICE OF THE LORD. MOSES FAILED TO SHIFT WHEN THE LORD SHIFTED.

DEUT 11:10-15 For the land, whither thou goest in to possess it, *is* not as the land of Egypt, from whence ye came out, where thou sowedst thy seed, and wateredst *it* with thy foot, as a garden of herbs:

11But the land, whither ye go to possess it, *is* a land of hills and valleys, *and* drinketh water of the rain of heaven:

12A land which the LORD thy God careth for: the eyes of the LORD thy God *are* always upon it, from the beginning of the year even unto the end of the year. **WHERE GOD ASSUMES FULL RESPONSIBILITY, BECAUSE WE TRUST AND OBEY HIM.**

13And it shall come to pass, if ye shall **hearken diligently** unto my commandments which I command you this day, to love the LORD your God, and to serve him with all your heart and with all your soul, **A LIFESTYLE OF OBEDIENCE, TRUE WORSHIP**

14That I will give *you* the rain of your land in his due season, the first rain and the latter rain, that thou mayest gather in thy corn, and thy wine, and thine oil.

15And I will send grass in thy fields for thy cattle, that thou mayest eat and be full.

SO MOSES QUESTIONS THE LORD ABOUT WHO WILL GO WITH HIM TO POSSESS THE PROMISED LAND. **EX 33:11** And the LORD spake unto Moses face to face, as a man speaketh unto his friend. And he turned again into the camp: but his servant **Joshua,** the son of Nun, a young man, departed not out of the tabernacle.

EX 33:12-14 And Moses said unto the LORD, See, thou sayest unto me, Bring up this people: and thou hast not **let me KNOW** whom thou wilt send with me. Yet thou hast said, I know thee by name, and thou hast also found grace in my sight.

13 Now therefore, I pray thee, **if** I have found grace in thy sight, shew me now thy way, **that I may KNOW** thee, that I may find grace in thy sight: and consider that this nation *is* thy people.

MOSES WANTED TO MOVE FROM QUESTIONING TO **KNOWING.** IN THIS PLACE OF KNOWING COMES **CONFIDENCE.**THE LORD WAS NOT SPEAKING WITH MOSES AS MUCH AS WHEN HE SENT HIM TO PHAROAH. THERE WERE NO PHYSICAL DEMONSTRATIONS AS AT THE BEGINNING, AND IT'S MAKING MOSES NERVOUS , RESTLESS. **The more we grow up in the Lord the less details He gives us. He trust that we have learned His ways and if we veer off course he redirects us.** Moses continues to pressure the Lord for more details

EX 33:15-23 And he said unto him, If thy presence go not *with me*, carry us not up hence.

16 For wherein shall it be known here that I and thy people have found grace in thy sight? *is it* not in that thou goest with us? so shall we be

separated, I and thy people, from all the people that *are* upon the face of the earth.

17 And the LORD said unto Moses, I will do this thing also that thou hast spoken: for thou hast found grace in my sight, and I know thee by name.

18 And he said, I beseech thee, **shew me** thy glory. MOSES WANTED A **DEMONSTRATION.**

19And he said, I will make all my goodness pass **before** thee, (**HIS WORD**) and I will proclaim the name of the LORD before thee; and will be gracious to whom I will be gracious, and will shew mercy on whom I will shew mercy.

20 And he said, Thou canst not see my face: for there shall no man see me, and live. LOOKING AT HIS FACE , IS AS LOOKING AT THE PERFORMANCE, THE PROCESS. WE CAN'T LOOK AT THE WIND AND LIVE. IF WE LOOK AT IT, LIKE PETER WE TOO, WILL BEGAN TO FEAR AND FAINT.

21 And the LORD said, Behold, *there is* a place **by** me, and thou shalt **stand** upon a rock: (**THAT WHERE I AM, THERE WILL MY SERVANT BE ALSO, IN THE SPIRIT**)! THIS ROCK IS SYMBOLIC, MEANING HIS WORD. "ROCK" Revelation OF Christ Kingdom. TAKE A STAND, FIRMLY POSITION OURSELVES IN THE PLACE OF HIS SPIRIT

THE PLACE WAS BY HIM, JUST ENOUGH TO GET THEM OUT OF THE WAY OF WHAT HE NEEDED TO DO. NOT TOO, FAR FROM HIM; BUT OUT OF THE WAY; STILL IN HIS PRESENCE, BUT OUT OF HIS WAY!

22 And it shall come to pass, **while, (THE PERFORMANCE)** my glory passeth by, that I will put thee in a clift, (**THE SECRET PLACE**), of the rock, **REVELATION,** and will cover thee with my hand **while** I pass by, **UNTIL FINISHED**: THE CLIFT IS THE OPENING OF THE EYES OF OUR UNDERSTANDING, THE OPENING UP

OF REVELATION THAT WE MAY ABIDE IN IT, A HIDDEN PLACE, THE SECRET PLACE, THE PLACE OF KNOWING HOW THE STORY ENDS. AS WE SUBMIT TO THE REVEALED KNOWLEDGE, HUMBLING OURSELVES, WE ARE HUMBLING OURSELVES UNDER HIS MIGHTY HAND THAT HE CAN COVER US. **THIS IS TO PREVENT US FROM LOOKING AT THE PROCESS, THE WINDS OF CHANGE!**

23 And I will take away mine hand, and thou shalt see my back parts: but my face shall not be seen. **ALL WE SEE IS THE GLORY HE LEAVES BEHIND, NOT THE PROCESS!**

**THE ROCK Revelation Of Christ Kingdom, IS THE PLACE OF THE KNOWING! REVELATION BIRTHS CONFIDENCE, CONFIDENCE BIRTHS BOLDNESS AND BOLDNESS ALLOWS ACCESS , KEYS INTO HIS GRACE! God's Riches At Christ Expense, THE FINISHED WORK!!! REST!

So God says to us that if we BELIEVE his word, we then STAND in the place by him, out of the way, positioned to RECEIVE POWER. HUMBLED to ABIDE, DWELLING in the REVELATION, THE SECRET PLACE, that He can cover us, WHILE HE PERFORMS THE THING THAT IS APPOINTED UNTO US!

**** SO WHERE IS THIS SECRET PLACE? IT'S IN THE **REVELATION**, THE REVEALED KNOWLEDGE OF CHRIST KINGDOM. THE SECRET, THAT THE GATES OF HELL CAN NOT AND SHALL NOT PREVAIL!

2 CHRON. 20:16-17 Tomorrow go ye down against them: behold, they come up by the cliff of Ziz; and ye shall find them at the end of the brook, before the wilderness of Jeruel. **REVEALED KNOWLEDGE, "THE SECRET PLACE"**

17 Ye shall not *need* to fight in this *battle*: set yourselves, **GET IN POSITION**, stand ye *still*, **HUMBLE YOURSELF UNDER MY MIGHT HAND** and **SEE** the salvation of the LORD with you, O Judah

and Jerusalem: fear not, nor be dismayed; to morrow go out against them: for the LORD *will be* with you.

PS 91:14 And he said, My presence shall go *with thee*, and I will give thee **REST.**

Resolve **E**very **S**ituation **T**otally **REVELATION IS THE POWER TO LIVE IN THE RESOLVE!!! THE KEYS TO ENTER INTO REST!**

5 Thou shalt not be afraid for the terror by night; *nor* for the arrow *that*flieth by day;

6 *Nor* for the pestilence *that walketh* in darkness; *nor* for the destruction *that wasteth* at noonday.

7 A thousand shall fall at thy side, and ten thousand at thy right hand; *but* it shall not come nigh thee.

8 Only with thine eyes shalt thou behold and see the reward of the wicked.

9 Because thou hast made the LORD, *which is* my refuge, *even* the most High, thy habitation; **THY DWELLING PLACE!!**

I MUST LEARN TO LIVE IN THIS PLACE. EX 33:11 And the LORD spake unto Moses face to face, as a man speaketh unto his friend. And he turned again into the camp: **but his servant Joshua**, the son of Nun, a young man, **departed not out of the tabernacle.**

JOSHUA 1:8 This book of the law shall not depart out of thy mouth; but thou shalt **meditate therein day and night,** that thou mayest observe to do according to all that is written therein: for then thou shalt make thy way prosperous, and then thou shalt have good success. **HUMILITY POSITIONS ME IN THE SECRET PLACE BUT MEDITATION KEEPS ME THERE**

PS 9:10 There shall no evil befall thee, neither shall any plague come nigh thy dwelling.

11 For he shall give his angels charge over thee, to keep thee in all thy ways.

12 They shall bear thee up in *their* hands, lest thou dash thy foot against a stone.

13 Thou shalt tread upon the lion and adder: the young lion and the dragon shalt thou trample under feet.

14 Because he hath set his love upon me, therefore will I deliver him: I will set him on high, because he hath known my name.

15 He shall call upon me, and I will answer him: I *will be* with him in trouble; I will deliver him, and honour him.

16 With long life will I satisfy him, and shew him my salvation. **NO DEATH, NO DESTRUCTION, BUT ABUNDANT LIFE! IN THIS HOUR WHERE DEATH IS ALL AROUND WE MUST LEARN TO LIVE , ABIDE, DWELL IN THE SECRET PLACE.**

Living In The Secret Place

PSALM 91; JOHN 5:1-5

PS 91: 1-16 He that dwelleth in the secret place of the most High shall abide under the shadow of the Almighty.

***DWELLING:

JOSHUA 1: 8 This book of the law shall not depart out of thy mouth; but thou shalt **meditate therein** day and night, that thou mayest observe to do according to all that is written therein: for then thou shalt make thy way prosperous, and then thou shalt have good success. **IN ORDER TO DWELL, MEDITATION HAS TO BECOME OUR LIFESTYLE!**

JOHN 14:10 Believest thou not that I am in the Father, and the Father in me? the words that I speak unto you I speak not of myself: but the Father that dwelleth in me, he doeth the works.

***ABIDING:

JOHN 15:1-8 I am the true vine, and my Father is the husbandman.

2 Every branch in me that beareth not fruit he taketh away: and every *branch* that beareth fruit, he purgeth it, that it may bring forth more fruit.

3 Now ye are clean through the word which I have spoken unto you.

4 **Abide in me,** and I in you. As the branch cannot bear fruit of itself, except it abide in the vine; no more can ye, except ye abide in me.

5 I am the vine, ye *are* the branches: He that abideth in me, and I in him, the same bringeth forth much fruit: for without me ye can do nothing.

6 If a man abide not in me, he is cast forth as a branch, and is withered; and men gather them, and cast *them* into the fire, and they are burned.

7 If ye abide in me, and my words abide in you, ye shall ask what ye will, and it shall be done unto you.

8 Herein is my Father glorified, that ye bear much fruit; so shall ye be my disciples. **IN ORDER TO ABIDE, MY LIFE HAS TO BE HUMBLY, SUBMITTED TO THE WORD, THE VOICE OF GOD! IN **OBEDIENCE!!!!!!!**

***WHEN WE LEARN TO HUMBLE OURSELVES AND SUBMIT TO THE WILL/WORD OF GOD, BECOMING A DOER, WE THEN ENTER THE HOLY PLACE WHERE WE RECEIVE KEYS, REVELATION TO ENTER IN TO THE SECRET PLACE, GOD'S PRESENCE. BUT IT'S MY DAILY MEDITATIONS THAT **KEEPS** ME ABIDING IN THE SECRET PLACE, HIS PRESENCE. **A CONSTANT REMINDER.**

EPHESIANS 3: 12 In whom we have boldness and access with confidence by the faith of him.

ISAIAH 40:27-31 Why sayest thou, O Jacob, and speakest, O Israel, My way is hid from the LORD, and my judgment is passed over from my God?

28 Hast thou not known? hast thou not heard, *that* the everlasting God, the LORD, the Creator of the ends of the earth, fainteth not, neither is weary? *there is* no searching of his understanding. **GOD KNOWS THE ROOT OF ALL CAUSES! THE POWER IN HIS KNOWING AND CONFIDENCE IN HIS PLAN. HE KNOWS THE ENDING FROM THE BEGINNING!**

29 He giveth power to the faint; and to *them that have* no might he increaseth strength

30 Even the youths shall faint and be weary, and the young men shall utterly fall:

*31 But they that wait upon the LORD, **CONTINUE TO SERVE HIM**, shall renew *their* strength; **they shall mount up with wings as eagles**; they shall run, and not be weary; *and* they shall walk, and not faint. **SOARING, FROM THE PLACE OF REST. LIVING IN THE RESOLVE! WAITING IN GOD WHILE WAITING ON GOD! THE PLACE OF NO RETURN. NO LOOKING BACK BUT SETTING FACE LIKE A FLINT PRESSING FORWARD, EXPECTING A MIRACLE.**

EX 14:8-29 And the LORD hardened the heart of Pharaoh king of Egypt, and he pursued after the children of Israel: and the children of Israel went out with an high hand.

9 But the Egyptians pursued after them, all the horses *and* chariots of Pharaoh, and his horsemen, and his army, and overtook them encamping by the sea, beside Pihahiroth, before Baalzephon.

10 And when Pharaoh drew nigh, the children of Israel lifted up their eyes, and, behold, the Egyptians marched after them; and they were sore afraid: and the children of Israel cried out unto the LORD.

11 And they said unto Moses, Because *there were* no graves in Egypt, hast thou taken us away to die in the wilderness? wherefore hast thou dealt thus with us, to carry us forth out of Egypt?

12 *Is* not this the word that we did tell thee in Egypt, saying, Let us alone, that we may serve the Egyptians? For *it had been* better for us to serve the Egyptians, than that we should die in the wilderness.

13 And Moses said unto the people, Fear ye not, stand still, and see the salvation of the LORD, which he will shew to you today: for the Egyptians whom ye have seen today, ye shall see them again no more forever.

14 The LORD shall fight for you, and ye shall hold your peace.

15 And the LORD said unto Moses, Wherefore criest thou unto me? speak unto the children of Israel, **that they go forward:**

16 But lift thou up thy rod, **WORD OF GOD** and stretch out thine hand over the sea, and divide it: and the children of Israel shall go on dry *ground* through the midst of the sea.

17 And I, behold, **I will harden the hearts of the Egyptians**, and they shall follow them: and I will get me honour upon Pharaoh, and upon all his host, upon his chariots, and upon his horsemen.

18 And the Egyptians shall know that I *am* the LORD, when I have gotten me honour upon Pharaoh, upon his chariots, and upon his horsemen.

***19 And the angel of God, which went before the camp of Israel, removed and went behind them; **SHIFTED** and the pillar of the cloud went from before their face, and stood behind them: **SHIFTED**

20 And it came **between** the camp of the Egyptians and the camp of Israel; and it was a cloud and **darkness *to them*, but it gave light by night *to these*:** so that the one came **not near** the other all the night.

21 And Moses stretched out his hand over the sea; and the **LORD caused the sea to go *back* by a strong east wind all that night**, and made the sea dry *land*, and the waters were divided. **THE STORM CAME TO**

BLESS! JUST KNOW WHEN WE PUT A DEMAND ON GOD'S WORD, THE SPIRIT BEGINS TO MOVE, MANIFESTED BY THE WIND. WINDS OF CHANGE! IT IS THEN GOD EXPECTS US TO RELEASE HIS WORD, JUST AS HE DID IN

**GENESIS 1:1-3 In the beginning God created the heaven and the earth.

2 And the earth was without form, and void; and darkness *was* upon the face of the deep. And the **Spirit of God moved** upon the face of the waters.

3 And **God said,** Let there be light: and there was light. **GOD RELEASED HIS WORD IN THE WIND SPIRIT!**

**AS SOON AS THE WORD GOETH FORTH OUT OF HIS MOUTH, IT BEGINS TO BE, BECOMING WHAT IT IS SENT TO ACCOMPLISH! STARTS IT'S PROCESS OF BECOMING!

22 And the children of Israel went into the midst of the sea upon the dry *ground*: and the waters *were* a wall unto them on their right hand, and on their left.

23 And the Egyptians pursued, and went in after them to the midst of the sea, *even* all Pharaoh's horses, his chariots, and his horsemen.

24 And it came to pass, that in the morning watch the LORD looked unto the host of the Egyptians **through** the pillar of fire and of the cloud, and troubled the host of the Egyptians,

25 And took off their chariot wheels, that they drave them heavily: so that the Egyptians said, Let us flee from the face of Israel; for the LORD fighteth for them against the Egyptians.

26 And the LORD said unto Moses, Stretch out thine hand over the sea, that the waters may come again upon the Egyptians, upon their chariots, and upon their horsemen.

27 And Moses stretched forth his hand over the sea, and the sea returned to his strength when the morning appeared; and the Egyptians fled against

it; and the LORD overthrew the Egyptians in the midst of the sea. **THE BATTLE IS THE LORDS!**

28 And the waters returned, and covered the chariots, and the horsemen, *and* all the host of Pharaoh that came into the sea after them; **there remained not so much as one of them.**

29 But the children of Israel walked upon dry *land* in the midst of the sea; and the waters *were* a wall unto them on their right hand, and on their left.

THE PERFORMANCE:

EXODUS 33:19 And he said, I will make all my goodness pass **before** thee, HIS WORD and I will proclaim the name of the LORD before thee; and will be gracious to whom I will be gracious, and will shew mercy on whom I will shew mercy.

20 And he said, Thou canst not see my face: for there shall no man see me, and live. LOOKING AT HIS FACE , IS AS LOOKING AT THE PERFORMANCE, THE PROCESS. WE CAN'T LOOK AT HE WIND OR FIRE AND LIVE. IF WE LOOK AT IT, LIKE PETER WE TOO WILL BEGAN TO FEAR AND FAINT.

21 And the LORD said, Behold, *there is* a place **by** me, and thou shalt **stand** upon a rock: **THAT WHERE I AM, THERE WILL MY SERVANT BE ALSO, IN THE SPIRIT!** THIS ROCK IS SYMBOLIC, MEANING HIS WORD. "ROCK" Revelation OF Christ Kingdom. TAKE A STAND, FIRMLY POSITION OURSELVES IN THE PLACE OF HIS SPIRIT

THE PLACE WAS BY HIM, JUST ENOUGH TO GET THEM OUT OF THE WAY OF WHAT HE NEEDED TO DO. NOT TOO, FAR FROM HIM; BUT OUT OF THE WAY; STILL IN HIS PRESENCE, BUT OUT OF HIS WAY!

22 And it shall come to pass, **while, (THE PERFORMANCE)** my glory passeth by, that I will put thee in a clift, (**THE SECRET PLACE**), of the rock, **REVELATION,** and will cover thee with my hand **while** I

pass by, **UNTIL FINISHED**: THE CLIFT IS THE OPENING OF THE EYES OF OUR UNDERSTANDING, THE OPENING UP OF REVELATION THAT WE MAY ABIDE IN IT , A HIDDEN PLACE, THE SECRET PLACE, THE PLACE OF KNOWING HOW THE STORY ENDS. AS WE SUBMIT TO THE REVEALED KNOWLEDGE, HUMBLE OURSELVES, WE ARE HUMBLING OURSELVES UNDER HIS MIGHTY HAND THAT HE CAN COVER US. **THIS IS TO PREVENT US FROM LOOKING AT THE PROCESS, THE WINDS OF CHANGE!**

23 And I will take away mine hand, and thou shalt see my back parts: but my face shall not be seen. **ALL WE SEE IS THE GLORY HE LEAVES BEHIND**

**THE ROCK Revelation Of Christ Kingdom, IS THE PLACE OF THE KNOWING! REVELATION BIRTHS CONFIDENCE, CONFIDENCE BIRTHS BOLDNESS AND BOLDNESS ALLOWS ACCESS , KEYS INTO HIS GRACE! God's Riches At Christ Expense, THE FINISHED WORK!!! REST

PRAYER FOR FOCUS:

FATHER thank you for your word. Teach me to hide it in my heart. I understand that your word is the transfer of your DNA and Power to me. When the enemy come to snatch it, Father help me by your power to stand, submit to you that I might resist him and put him on the run. Father, your desire is to have my heart. I understand that I give you my heart by believing and receiving your word. This enables you to sit on the throne of my heart to rule and reign. I understand there is a battle for who sits on the throne of my heart as Lord. I understand the power of words give access to my heart. I give my heart to only you. It is your voice that I will obey and follow. Just as Jesus gave His heart only to you, so do I; that we all can be one in you. Father, help me to not break the cycle of your word, but allow it to complete a work in and through me. Help me not to hinder the process, while you are performing the thing that is appointed unto me. Help me to remain in love that my faith be not hindered. Help me to recognize offense, so I will not allow my heart to be offended and hinder the flow of you Spirit in my life to receive. Thank you Father that your word is one size fits all; and it sanctifies us and keeps us from partaking in evil. It's only by your grace through faith I am saved, not of my works; therefore, I have nothing to boast about, I give you the glory for every change in my life, knowing without you I can do nothing.

In Jesus name, Amen.

"Resting In The Finished Work"

DAN 11:32 HEB 4:1-3

DAN 11:32 And such as do wickedly against the covenant shall he corrupt by flatteries: but the people that do know their God shall be strong, and do *exploits*.

POWER IS IN THE KNOWING! THE MOST POWERFUL PRAYER IS ONE THAT KNOWS ; PRAYING FROM THE FINISH WORK, IN CONFIDENCE, BOLDING MAKING A WITHDRAWAL. THEREBY PUTTING A DEMAND ON GOD'S WORD EXPECTING A SUPPLY!

JOHN 1:10-14 He was in the world, and the world was made by him, and the world knew him not.

11 He came unto his own, and his own received him not.

12 But as many as received him, to them gave he **power to become** the sons of God, *even* to them that believe on his name:

13 Which were born, not of blood, nor of the will of the flesh, nor of the will of man, but of God.

14 And the Word was made flesh, and dwelt among us, (and we beheld his glory, the glory as of the only begotten of the Father,) full of grace and truth.

THE POWER IS THE REVELATION, THE REVEALED KNOWLEDGE OF GOD!

MATT 16:13-19 When Jesus came into the coasts of Caesarea Philippi, he asked his disciples, saying, Whom do men say that I the Son of man am?

14 And they said, Some *say that thou art* John the Baptist: some, Elias; and others, Jeremias, or one of the prophets.

15 He saith unto them, But whom say ye that I am ?

16 And Simon Peter answered and said, Thou art the Christ, the Son of the living God.

17 And Jesus answered and said unto him, Blessed art thou, Simon Barjona: for flesh and blood hath not revealed *it* unto thee, but my Father which is in heaven.

18 And I say also unto thee, That thou art Peter, and upon this rock I will build my church; and the gates of hell shall not prevail against it.

19 And I will give unto thee the keys of the kingdom of heaven: and whatsoever thou shalt bind on earth shall be bound in heaven: and whatsoever thou shalt loose on earth shall be loosed in heaven

THE REVEALED KNOWLEDGE IN THE PLACE OF OUR KNOWING, PRODUCING CONFIDENCE. IT IS THE SECRETS THAT ARE REVEALED. **THE SECRET GIVES US THE ADVANTAGE, POWER, THAT TURNS THE TABLE.** THEREFORE WE CAN REST IN THE FINISHED WORK, WHAT'S ALREADY DONE.

SO IT MATTERS NOT WHAT WE SEE WITH OUR NATURAL EYE, **WHAT WE SEE WITH OUR SPIRITUAL EYE OVER RIDES IT. BECAUSE OF WHAT WE KNOW! KNOWLEDGE IS POWER!!!**

Revelation is the revealed knowledge of Christ Kingdom and the revealed knowledge is the Revelation of Christ Kingdom "ROCK". **KNOWING HOW THE KINGDOM OPERATES!**

IN THE PLACE OF THIS KNOWEDGE. REVELATION,SECRET, WE CAN FIND REST IF WE MIXED THE WORD OF GOD WITH FAITH.

HEB 4:1-3 Let us therefore fear, lest, a promise being left *us* of entering into his rest, any of you should seem to come short of it.

2 For unto us was the gospel preached, as well as unto them: but the word preached did not profit them, not being mixed with faith in them that heard *it*.

3 For we which have believed do enter into rest, as he said, As I have sworn in my wrath, if they shall enter into my rest: **although the works were finished from the foundation of the world.**

POWER IS IN THE REVEALED KNOWLEDGE, **THE REVELATION THAT IT'S ALREADY DONE!** THIS CHANGES OUR POSITION AND APPROACH IN PRAYER. WE PRAY FROM VICTORY. NOT WORRY OR TRYING TO FIGURE OUT HOW GOD BRINGS IT TO PASS, BUT DESIRING TO **KNOW WHERE THE OPEN DOOR IS, KNOWING IT'S ALREADY DONE!**

MATT 7:7 Ask, and it shall be given you; seek, and ye shall find; knock, and it shall be opened unto you:

1 PETER 1:3-9;13-19 Blessed *be* the God and Father of our Lord Jesus Christ, which according to his abundant mercy hath begotten us again unto a lively hope by the resurrection of Jesus Christ from the dead,

4 To an inheritance incorruptible, and undefiled, and that fadeth not away, reserved in heaven for you, **RESERVED IN HEAVEN (THE WAREHOUSE) ALREADY DONE!**

5 Who are kept by the **POWER of God** (WORD) through faith unto salvation ready to be revealed in the last time.

ECC 8:4 Where the word of a king *is, there is* power: and who may say unto him, What doest thou? **PUTTING A DEMAND ON GOD'S WORD MIXING IT WITH FAITH. "THE TRANSACTION"

6 Wherein ye greatly rejoice, though now for a season, if need be, ye are in heaviness through manifold temptations:

7 That the trial of your faith, being much more precious than of gold that perisheth, though it be tried with fire, might be found unto praise and honour and glory at the appearing of Jesus Christ:

8 Whom having not seen, ye love; in whom, though now ye see *him* not, yet believing, ye rejoice with joy unspeakable and full of glory: **"THE TRANSITION"**

9 **Receiving** the end of your faith, *even* the salvation of *your* souls.

13 Wherefore gird up the loins of your mind, **(STOP TRIPPIN),** be sober, **(DON'T DOUBT OR WAVER)** and hope, **(STAY IN CONFIDENCE),** to the end, for the grace that is to be **brought** unto you, **(OVER TAKE YOU),** at the revelation, **(THE POSITION AND PLACE OF YOUR REST, RESOLVE AND CONFIDENCE)** of Jesus Christ;

**HEB 10:35 Cast not away therefore your confidence, which hath great recompence of reward.

THE PROCESS FROM TRANSACTION TO TRANSITION IS TO PREPARE US TO RECEIVE AND MAINTAIN. 6 Wherein ye greatly rejoice, though now for a season, if need be, ye are in heaviness through manifold temptations:

7 That the trial of your faith, being much more precious than of gold that perisheth, though it be tried with fire, (**TO RID IMPURITIES, MIND**

SETS) might be found unto praise and honour and glory at the appearing of Jesus Christ:

THE PROMISE MUST COME THROUGH A HOLY AND RIGHTEOUS WOMB. WHAT IS CONCEIVED IN RIGHTEOUSNESS, FAITH BELIEVING AND TRUSTING GOD, HIS WORD; MUST BE BORN INTO A HOLY ENVIRONMENT TO BE SUSTAINED.

14 As obedient children, not fashioning yourselves according to the former lusts in your ignorance:

15 But as he which hath called you is holy, so be ye holy in all manner of conversation;

16 Because it is written, Be ye holy; for I am holy.

DEUT 11:10-21 For the land, whither thou goest in to possess it, *is* not as the land of Egypt, from whence ye came out, where thou sowedst thy seed, and wateredst *it* with thy foot, as a garden of herbs:

11 But the land, whither ye go to possess it, *is* a land of hills and valleys, *and* drinketh water of the rain of heaven:

12 A land which the LORD thy God careth for: the eyes of the LORD thy God *are* always upon it, from the beginning of the year even unto the end of the year.

13 And it shall come to pass, if ye shall hearken diligently unto my commandments which I command you this day, to love the LORD your God, and to serve him with all your heart and with all your soul,

PETER 1:15 But as he which hath called you is holy, so be ye holy in **all manner of conversation; (**MIND, WILL, EMOTIONS, IMAGINATION, DESIRES)**

14 That I will give *you* the rain of your land in his due season, the first rain and the latter rain, that thou mayest gather in thy corn, and thy wine, and thine oil.

15 And I will send grass in thy fields for thy cattle, that thou mayest eat and be full. **PROVISION FOR ALL!**

2 CORN 9:7-8 Every man according as he purposeth in his heart, *so let him give*; not grudgingly, or of necessity: for God loveth a cheerful giver.

8 And God *is* able to make all grace abound toward you; that ye, always having all sufficiency in all *things*, may abound to every good work:

16 Take heed to yourselves, that your heart be not deceived, and ye turn aside, and serve other gods, and worship them;

17 And *then* the LORD'S wrath be kindled against you, and he shut up the heaven, that there be no rain, and that the land yield not her fruit; and *lest* ye perish quickly from off the good land which the LORD giveth you.

18 Therefore shall ye lay up these my words in your heart and in your soul, and bind them for a sign upon your hand, that they may be as frontlets between your eyes.

19 And ye shall teach them your children, speaking of them when thou sittest in thine house, and when thou walkest by the way, when thou liest down, and when thou risest up. **GOD IS TRYING TO ESTABLISH IN AND THROUGH US A GENERATIONAL BLESSING, INHERITANCE.**

20 And thou shalt write them upon the door posts of thine house, and upon thy gates:

21 That your days may be multiplied, and the days of your children, in the land which the LORD sware unto your fathers to give them, as the days of heaven upon the earth. **ABIDING IN THE BLESSING, PROMISE.**

"The Goodness Of My Affliction"

EX. 1:8-12 Now there arose up a new king over Egypt, which knew not Joseph.

9 And he said unto his people, Behold, the people of the children of Israel *are* more and mightier than we:

10 Come on, let us deal wisely with them; lest they multiply, and it come to pass, that, when there falleth out any war, they join also unto our enemies, and fight against us, and *so* get them up out of the land.

11 Therefore they did set over them taskmasters to afflict them with their burdens. And they built for Pharaoh treasure cities, Pithom and Raamses.

12 But the more they afflicted them, the more they multiplied and grew. And they were grieved because of the children of Israel. BELIEVE IT OR NOT THERE IS A BLESSING IN THE AFFLICTION.

PS.119:71 *It is* **good for me that I have been** **afflicted; that I might learn thy statutes.**

"THE PROBLEM"

Afflictions have a way of pushing us into the presence of the Lord. When God allows this, its only and always to bring us closer to him; a way of bringing order and to our lives; a process for pruning, a place of strength when weak. Where Pain is the sign of weakness leaving our bodies. To a place where his will becomes our will, through our willingness to trust and OBEY HIM. The affliction brings us to a place of agreement ******AMOS 3:3 Can two walk together, except they be agreed?** Oneness, Unity with God, his Spirit and His word.

THE AFFLICTION IS THE DRESSING ROOM WHERE GARMENTS ARE CHANGED. WHERE WE TAKE OFF

THE WORKS OF THE FLESH AND PUT ON THE ROBE OF RIGHTEOUSNESS.

PS. 34:19 Many *are* the afflictions of the righteous: but the LORD delivereth him out of them all.

AS A RESULT OF MY CHOICES, BEING THE LORDS ROD OF CORRECTION, OR APPOINT UNTO , THE LORDS PROCESS FOR PREPARATION , BOTH END IN DEATH AND A NEW BEGINNING.

***** ISRAEL'S CHOICES SELF- INFLICTED**

EX. 2:23-25 And it came to pass in process of time, that the king of Egypt died: and the children of Israel sighed by reason of the bondage, and they cried, and their cry came up unto God by reason of the bondage.

24 And God heard their groaning, and God remembered his covenant with Abraham, with Isaac, and with Jacob.

25 And God looked upon the children of Israel, and God had respect unto *them.*

SOMETIMES THE LORD USES THE AFFLICTION AS A ROD OF CORRECTION TO TURN OUR HEARTS BACK TO HIM.

EX. 3:7-10 And the LORD said, I have surely **seen the affliction** of my people which *are* in Egypt, and have **heard their cry** by reason of their taskmasters; for I **know their <u>sorrows</u>; THERE HAS BEEN A CHANGE OF HEART!**

"THE PROMISE"

8 And I am come down to deliver them out of the hand of the Egyptians, and to bring them up out of that land unto a good land and a large, **unto a land flowing with milk and honey; TO BRING THEM OUT OF EGYPT INTO MY KINGDOM!** unto the place of the Canaanites, and

the Hittites, and the Amorites, and the Perizzites, and the Hivites, and the Jebusites. **WHERE THE WEALTH OF THE WICKED.**

NUMBERS 14:19 THEY BE BREAD FOR US, PROVISION!

PS. 66:12 Thou hast caused men to ride over our heads; we went through fire and through water: but thou broughtest us out into a wealthy *place*.

9 Now therefore, behold, the cry of the children of Israel is come unto me: and I have also seen the oppression wherewith the Egyptians oppress them.

"THE PROPHET/POWER"

10 Come now therefore, and I will send thee unto Pharaoh, that thou mayest bring forth my people the children of Israel out of Egypt."

HOSEA 12:13 And by a prophet the LORD brought Israel out of Egypt, and by a prophet was he preserved.

EX. 2:24 And God heard their <u>groaning</u>, and God remembered his covenant

ROM 8:22 For we know that the whole creation groaneth and travaileth in pain together until now. BIRTHING THE KINGDOM OF GOD, HIS RIGHTEOUSNESS.

THE AFFLICTION PRODUCES THE OUTCOME INTENDED.

"THE PURPOSE"

HEB. 12:11 Now no chastening " **THE ROD OF CORRECTION"** for the present seemeth to be joyous, but grievous: nevertheless afterward it **yieldeth the peaceable fruit of righteousness unto them which are exercised thereby.**

THEN THERE ARE APPOINTED AFFLICTIONS, DESIGNED BY THE LORD TO PRUNE FOR BARING MORE FRUIT AND TO PREPARE FOR GREATER ASSIGNMENTS, ALLOWED OF THE

LORD TO EVEN ENCOURAGE OTHERS AND BRING GLORY TO HIS NAME. SUFFERING FOR RIGHTEOUSNESS SAKE.

1 THESS. 3:2-3 And sent Timotheus, our brother, and minister of God, and our fellow labourer in the gospel of Christ, to establish you, and to comfort you concerning your faith:

3 That no man should be moved by these afflictions: for yourselves know that we are appointed thereunto.

1 THESS 2: 2-17 For yourselves, brethren, know our entrance in unto you, that it was not in vain:

2 But even after that we had suffered before, and were shamefully entreated, as ye know, at Philippi, we were bold in our God to speak unto you the gospel of God with much contention.

3 For our exhortation *was* not of deceit, nor of uncleanness, nor in guile:

4 But as we were allowed of God to be put in trust with the gospel, even so we speak; not as pleasing men, **but God, which trieth our hearts.**

5 For neither at any time used we flattering words, as ye know, nor a cloke of covetousness; God *is* witness:

6 Nor of men sought we glory, neither of you, nor *yet* of others, when we might have been burdensome, as the apostles of Christ.

7 But we were gentle among you, even as a nurse cherisheth her children:

8 So being affectionately desirous of you, we were willing to have imparted unto you, not the gospel of God only, but also our own souls, because ye were dear unto us.

9 For ye remember, brethren, our labour and travail: for labouring night and day, because we would not be chargeable unto any of you, we preached unto you the gospel of God.

10 Ye *are* witnesses, and God *also*, how holily and justly and unblameably we behaved ourselves among you that believe:

11 As ye know how we exhorted and comforted and charged every one of you, as a father *doth* his children,

12 That ye would walk worthy of God, who hath called you unto his kingdom and glory.

13 For this cause also thank we God without ceasing, because, when ye received the word of God which ye heard of us, ye received *it* not *as* the word of men, but as it is in truth, the word of God, **which effectually worketh** also in you that believe.

14 For ye, brethren, became followers of the churches of God which in Judaea are in Christ Jesus: for ye also have suffered like things of your own countrymen, even as they *have* of the Jews:

15 Who both killed the Lord Jesus, and their own prophets, and have persecuted us; and they please not God, and are contrary to all men:

16 Forbidding us to speak to the Gentiles that they might be saved, to fill up their sins alway: for the wrath is come upon them to the uttermost.

17 But we, brethren, being taken from you for a short time in presence, not in heart, endeavoured the more abundantly to see your face with great desire.

18 Wherefore we would have come unto you, even I Paul, once and again; but Satan hindered us.

"THE PROCESS"

PHIL 3:7-15 But what things were gain to me, those I counted loss for Christ.

8 Yea doubtless, and I count all things *but* loss for the excellency of the knowledge of Christ Jesus my Lord: for whom I have suffered the loss of all things, and do count them *but* dung, that I may win Christ,

9 And be **found in him, not having mine own righteousness**, which is of the law, but that which is through the faith of Christ, **the righteousness which is of God by faith:**

10 That I may know him, and the power of his resurrection, and the fellowship of his sufferings, being made conformable unto his death;

11 If by any means I might attain unto the resurrection of the dead.

12 Not as though I had already attained, either were already perfect: but I follow after, if that I may apprehend that for which also I am apprehended of Christ Jesus.

13 Brethren, I count not myself to have apprehended: but *this* one thing *I do*, forgetting those things which are behind, and reaching forth unto those things which are before,

14 I press toward the mark for the prize of the high calling of God in Christ Jesus. **SET HIS FACE LIKE A FLINT DETERMINED TO FINISH AND NOT LOOK BACK NO MATTER WHAT THE COST COUNTING THE COST.**

15 Let us therefore, as many as be perfect, be thus minded: and if in any thing ye be otherwise minded, God shall reveal even this unto you.

JESUS WAS APPOINTED UNTO AFFLICTIONS, PLEASED THE FATHER BEING BEATEN AND MARRED. **BUT THE FATHER TAKES FULL RESPONSIBILITY FOR WHAT HE ALLOWS!**

THERE IS PURPOSE BEHIND THE PAIN

1 THESS 1:3-10 Blessed *be* God, even the Father of our Lord Jesus Christ, the Father of mercies, and the God of all comfort;

4 Who comforteth us in all our tribulation, **(AFFLICTIONS) that we may be able (EQUIPPED) to comfort them which are in any trouble, by the comfort wherewith we ourselves are comforted of God.**

5 For as the sufferings of Christ abound in us, so our consolation also aboundeth by Christ.

6 And whether we be afflicted, *it is* **for your consolation and salvation**, which is **effectual** in the enduring of the same sufferings which we also suffer: or whether we be comforted, *it is* for your consolation and salvation. **PRODUCED THE OUTCOME INTENDED TO DO WHAT IS REQUIRED,** PAY IT FORWARD!

7 **And our hope of you** *is* **stedfast, knowing, that as ye are partakers of the sufferings, so** *shall ye be* **also, of the consolation.**

8 For we would not, brethren, have you ignorant of our trouble which came to us in Asia, that we were pressed out of measure, above strength, insomuch that we despaired even of life:

9 **But we had the sentence of death in ourselves**, that we should not trust in ourselves, **but in God** which raiseth the dead: (REST) TRUE RIGHTEOUSNESS

10 Who **delivered** us from so great a death, and doth deliver: in whom we trust that he will yet deliver *us*;

FLESH DYING THAT THE SPIRIT MIGHT LIVE IN ME

GAL 2:20-21 I am crucified with Christ: nevertheless I live; yet not I, but Christ liveth in me: and the life which I now live in the flesh I live by the faith of the Son of God, who loved me, and gave himself for me. [21]**I do not frustrate the grace of God: for if righteousness** *come* **by the law, then Christ is dead in vain**

"THE PERFECTION"

But we have this treasure in earthen vessels, that the excellency of the power may be of God, and not of us.

8 *We are* troubled on every side, yet not distressed; *we are* perplexed, but not in despair;

9 Persecuted, but not forsaken; cast down, but not destroyed;

10 Always bearing about in the body the dying of the Lord Jesus, that the life also of Jesus might be made manifest in our body.

11 For we which live are alway delivered unto death for Jesus' sake, that the life also of Jesus might be made manifest in our mortal flesh.

12 So then death worketh in us, but life in you.

13 We having the same spirit of faith, according as it is written, I believed, and therefore have I spoken; we also believe, and therefore speak;

14 Knowing that he which raised up the Lord Jesus shall raise up us also by Jesus, and shall present *us* with you.

15 For all things *are* for your sakes, that the abundant grace might through the thanksgiving of many redound to the glory of God.

16 For which cause we faint not; but though our outward man perish, yet the inward *man* is renewed day by day.

17 For our light affliction, which is but for a moment, worketh for us a far more exceeding *and* eternal weight of glory;

18 While we look not at the things which are seen, but at the things which are not seen: for the things which are seen *are* temporal; but the things which are not seen *are* eternal. TO REVEAL THE HIDDEN TREASURE IN MY EARTHEN VESSEL.

LUKE 22:31-34 And the Lord said, Simon, Simon, behold, Satan hath desired *to have* you, that he may sift *you* as wheat:

32 But I have prayed for thee, that thy faith fail not: and when thou art converted, strengthen thy brethren.

33 And he said unto him, Lord, I am ready to go with thee, both into prison, and to death. AND THIS IS WHAT WE HAVE SAID

34 And he said, I tell thee, Peter, the cock shall not crow this day, before that thou shalt thrice deny that thou knowest me. BUT THIS IS WHAT MANY OF US HAVE DONE. PETER WAS PROCESSED FOR PURPOSE AND THERE WAS A PURPOSE FOR THE PROCESS. A **SIFTING IN THE SHIFTING**

FROM THE FOUNDATION OF THE WORLD (HEB. 4:3B)HE KNEW COVID WOULD BE HERE AND ITS ON SCHEDULE, ECC 3:1, (PROV 16:4) HATH MADE ALL THINGS FOR HIMSELF, THE EVIL MAN FOR THE EVIL DAY. BUT THIS AFFLICTION COMES WITH AN ASSIGNMENT , THERE IS A PURPOSE FOR THIS PROCESS AND THE PROCESS IS FOR PURPOSE. TO **PURIFY AND TURN** THE HEARTS OF THE PEOPLE BACK TO HIM. GOD IS NOT MOCKED, WHATSOEVER A MAN SOWETH, THAT SHALL HE ALSO REAP.

1 THESS 2:4 Paul at Phillipi said it was not about pleasing men, **but God, which trieth our hearts.**

IT WAS GOOD THAT I HAD BEEN AFFLICTED!

"A Vessel Fit For The Masters Use"

DANIEL 1:1-4; 8-9   2 TIM. 2:19-21

DANIEL 1:1-4; 8-9 In the third year of the reign of Jehoiakim king of Judah came Nebuchadnezzar king of Babylon unto Jerusalem, and besieged it.

2 And the Lord gave Jehoiakim king of Judah into his hand, with part of the vessels of the house of God: which he carried into the land of Shinar to the house of his god; and he brought the vessels into the treasure house of his god.

3 And the king spake unto Ashpenaz the master of his eunuchs, that he should bring *certain* of the children of Israel, and of the king's seed, and of the princes;

4 Children in whom *was* **no blemish, but well favoured, and skilful in all wisdom, and cunning in knowledge, and understanding science, and such as** *had* **ability in them to stand in the king's palace,** and whom they might teach the learning and the tongue of the Chaldeans.

8 But Daniel **purposed in his hear**t that he would not defile himself with the portion of the king's meat, nor with the wine which he drank: therefore he requested of the prince of the eunuchs that he might not defile himself.

9 Now God had brought Daniel into favour and tender love with the prince of the eunuchs.

We live in a time where the people of God have gotten so caught up on positions and titles. People want to be used of God, But not all want to live Holy. What good is the position or title if we are not equipped for service; ill prepared for the assignment. Because with a position or title comes responsibilities. We must be able to do the work and sometimes the work can be challenging. Having to endure many afflictions , FOR THE PURPOSE OF ESTABLISHING THE KINGDOM OF GOD IN THE EARTH. EVEN NOW THE AFFLICTIONS THAT WE ARE YET HAVING TO ENDURE, IS OPPORTUNITY TO ESTABLISH GOD'S KINGDOM.

2 TIM. 2:19-21 Nevertheless the foundation of God (PROCESS) standeth sure, having this seal, The Lord knoweth them that are his. And, Let everyone that nameth the name of Christ depart from iniquity.

20 But in a great house there are not only vessels of gold and of silver, but also of wood and of earth; and some to honour, and some to dishonour.

21 If a man therefore purges himself from these, he shall be a vessel unto honour, sanctified, and meet for the master's use, *and* prepared unto every good work. PREPARED FOR EVERY GOOD WORK. NOT

LIMITED TO A PODIUM OR PULPIT. MINISTRY IS EVERYDAY LIFE! THAT'S WHY HOLINESS IS A LIFESTYLE, WHERE THERE CAN BE NO WILLFUL SIN PERMITTED. **ROM 6:11-12** Likewise reckon ye also yourselves to be dead indeed unto sin, but alive unto God through Jesus Christ our Lord. **12** Let not sin therefore reign in your mortal body, that ye should obey it in the lusts thereof.

No matter what the assignment is we will be prepared and equipped , But only when we depart from iniquity. Its in the heat of the assignment, where we really find out what's in us.

Here we find Daniel and the 3 Hebrew boys as we know them starting their process for promotion, little did they know what was ahead. But the bible says that they were CHOSEN VESSELS, and although man looks at the outer, God looks at the heart.

4 Children in whom *was* **no blemish, but well favoured, and skilful in all wisdom, and cunning in knowledge, and understanding science, and such as *had* ability in them to stand in the king's palace,** and whom they might teach the learning and the tongue of the Chaldeans.

I HAVE LEARNED THAT EVERYTHING DOESN'T SHOW UP EVEN IN BACKGROUND CHECKS. SKILLFUL IN ALL WISDOM, CUNNING IN KNOWLEDGE, AND UNDERSTAND THE SCIENCE, BUT CRAZY AS ALL GET OUT, BACKWARDS, AS MY GRANDMA WOULD SAY, AS 2 LEFT SHOES. FEAR, ANXIETY, PROCRASTINATION,JEALOUSY,ENVY, GOSSIP, YOUTHFUL LUST AND STRIFE. THESE CAN'T BE SEE ON THE SURFACE. AND IF GOD HAS NOT PROCESSED US, THEY WILL CAUSE US TO ABORT OUR ASSIGNMENT. **SEE OUR GIFT MAY MAKE ROOM TO GET US THERE, BUT IT'S OUR CHARACTER THAT KEEPS US THERE.** THIS IS WHY WHEN GOD IS DEALING WITH AN AREA OF OUR LIVES, WE MUST SURRENDER TO THE PROCESS. EVERY STEP IS CRUCIAL.*WHEN baking a cake, all the ingredients are there, but if not allowed to stay the set time in the oven, IT WILL FALL IN THE MIDDLE AFTER COOLING. THAT'S YOU AND I. **AND IF WE'RE WONDERING WHY WE**

KEEP GOING AROUND THE SAME MOUNTAIN, ITS BECAUSE WE ARE NOT ALLOWING GOD TO HAVE HIS WAY IN THE PROCESS, RESISTING THE PROCESS, WHEN WE NEED TO BE RESISTING THE DEVIL.

DON'T PLAY WITH THE PROCESS, IT HAS A PURPOSE!! AND IN THAT PURPOSE IS OUR PROVISION.

**DON'T MESS UP THE FAVOR OF GOD!

IF we have been in the fire and allowed it to produce a finished work in us then we are fireproof. IT HAS PRODUCED THE OUTCOME INTENDED, TO DO WHAT IS REQUIRED. FULLY EQUIPPED. So we must allow the process to bring our iniquities to the surface and then deal with them, so that we may be able to STAND when under fire from the assignment.

4 Children in whom *was* **no blemish, but well favoured, and skilful in all wisdom, and cunning in knowledge, and understanding science, and such as** *had the ability* **in them to stand in the king's palace,** and whom they might teach the learning and the tongue of the Chaldeans.

STAND. The problem arises due to our decision to stand. 8 But Daniel **purposed in his hear**t that he would not defile himself with the portion of the king's meat, nor with the wine which he drank: therefore he requested of the prince of the eunuchs that he might not defile himself. WE WILL NOT CHANGE WHAT WE CONFORM TO. THE REASON JESUS ENDURED SO MUCH PERSECUTION IS BECAUSE HE REFUSE TO CONFORM, BY HIM NOT WILLING TO COMPROMISE, HE EXPOSED THAT THEIR DEEDS, THEIR SYSTEMS WERE CORRUPT, EVIL. **HE DID NOT COME TO CONFORM, BUT TO CHANGE AND TAKE OVER!**

(ROM 12:1-2) I beseech you therefore, brethren, by the mercies of God, that ye present your bodies a living sacrifice, holy, acceptable unto God, *which is* your reasonable service.

2 And **be not conformed** to this world: but be ye transformed by the renewing of your mind, that ye may **prove what** *is* **that good, and acceptable, and perfect, will of God.** JESUS STOOD AND THE FATHER DID THE WORK

JOHN 14:10 Believest thou not that I am in the Father, and the Father in me? the words that I speak unto you I speak not of myself: b**ut the Father that dwelleth in me, he doeth the works.**

3 For I say, through the **grace given unto me**, to every man that is among you, not to think *of himself* **more highly** than he ought to think; but to think **soberly**, according as God hath dealt to every man the measure of faith. **PRIDE,** WILL CAUSE US TO TRY TO DO WHAT WE KNOW WE CAN'T DO. **LUST,** LURING US OVER A CLIFT TO FALL, NOW WE'RE IN **COMPETITION,** FINDING OURSELVES IN A **PLACE OF CONFORMING,** LURED INTO THE GAME.

But Daniel purposed in his heart. **Living life on purpose, by purpose for purpose; not willing to compromise, conform no matter what the cost. HIS HEART WAS FIXED AND HIS MIND MADE UP, THAT HE WOULD NOT BE DEFILED!**

JOHN 14: 30-31 Hereafter I will not talk much with you: for the prince of this world cometh, and hath **nothing in me.** NO RESIDUE, SOLD OUT, NOT IN ME TO BE TEMPTED. FORSAKING ALL. **NO TRUMP CARDS, NO FEAR!**

31 But that the **world may know that I love the Father**; and as the Father gave me commandment, even so I do. **WILL OBEY**Arise, let us go hence. **LOVE, KEPT HIS COMMANDMENTS.**

DANIEL in a place of FAVOR AND TENDER LOVE Tender because although he was tight with the Lead supervisor he was not yet in good with the owner.

GOD KNOWS IF HE CAN TRUST US WITH THE ASSIGNMENT, IT'S NOT ABOUT US, BUT THAT GOD CAN USE US TO POSESS

THE LAND FOR THE KINGDOM. ADVANCING THE KINGDOM OF GOD.

*****AFFLICTIONS PREPARE US FOR ASSIGNMENTS!!!

10) And the prince of the eunuchs said unto Daniel, **I fear my lord the king, guess what? DAVID FEARED HIS LORD TOO)** who hath appointed your meat and your drink: **(DAVID HUNGERED AND THIRST AFTER RIGHTEOUSNESS, THERE WAS NO APPETITE FOR WHAT HE HAD TO OFFER) watchout for those unhealthy appetites. THE ENEMY KNOWS THAT WITH DESIRE COMES APPETITE. DON'T LET IT COST YOU YOUR INHERITANCE. The KING PROMISED GREAT RICHES TO THE MAN THAT COULD DESTROY GOLIATH!** for why should he see your faces worse than the children which *are* of your sort? then shall ye make *me* **endanger** my head to the king.

HERE DANIEL HAS AN **OPPORTUNITY** TO EITHER WIN A SOUL FOR THE KINGDOM OR COMPROMISE FOR THE SAKE OF HIS INFLUENCE, AND MESS UP HIS FAVOR. **REMEMBER THIS IS A KINGDOM ASSIGNMENT AND ITS ALL TO GLORIFY OUR FATHER IN HEAVEN. MY FAVOR IS PREDICATED ON MY OBEDIENCE. IT MAY NOT BE FAIR, BUT IT IS JUST!**

ALTHOUGH THE EUNUCH WAS AFRAID, **DANIEL WAS NOT TROUBLED AND HAD ENOUGH FAITH FOR THE BOTH OF THEM. ARE YOU ABLE TO CARRY THE WEAK IN FAITH? IT COMES WITH THE ASSIGNMENT.**

ROM. 15:1 We then that are strong ought to bear the infirmities of the weak, and not to please ourselves.

ROM. 14:1 Him that is weak in the faith receive ye, *but* not to doubtful disputations.

**YOUR OPPORTUNITY TO COMPROMISE IS CALCULATED IN THE FAVOR, DON'T DO IT. FAVOR COMES WITH PROTECTION.

15) And at the end of ten days their countenances appeared **fairer and fatter** in flesh than all the children which did eat the portion of the king's meat.

16 Thus Melzar took away the portion of their meat, and the wine that they **should drink**; and **gave them pulse.** (all the children which did eat) **CHANGED THE SYSTEM!**

17) **As for these four children, God gave them knowledge and skill in all learning and wisdom: and Daniel had understanding in all visions and dreams.** GOD REWARDS OBEDIENCE. **THE ANOINTING COST! (4)** whom **they might teach** BUT GOD! the learning and the tongue of the Chaldeans. **1 CORN 3:21** Therefore let no man glory in men. **For all things are yours;**

***REVELATION ONLY COMES BY WAY OF RELATIONSHIP!**

19-20) And the king **communed with them**; (RESPECT GAINED) and among them all was found none like Daniel, Hananiah, Mishael, and Azariah: therefore **stood** they before the king. **GOD PROMOTED THEM, THEY STOOD BECAUSE DANIEL TOOK A STAND. GREAT LEADERS LEAD BY EXAMPLE.**

20 And **in all matters of wisdom *and* understanding,** that the king enquired of them, he found them ten times better than all the magicians *and* astrologers that *were* in all his realm. ***DOORS GOD OPEN, NO MAN CAN CLOSE, WHEN WE OBEY AND NOT COMPROMISE.**

ROM. 8:28-39 And we know that all things work together **for good (CAN'T BE ALTERED)** to them that love God, to them who are the called according to *his* purpose.

29 For whom he did **foreknow**, he also did **predestinate** *to be* conformed to the **image of his Son**, that he might be the firstborn among many brethren.

30 Moreover whom he did predestinate, them he also **called**: and whom he called, them he also **justified**: and whom he justified, them he also **glorified**.

31 What shall we then say to these things? **If God** *be* **for us, who** *can be* **against** us? **THE BATTLE IS THE LORDS, THE FATHER DOETH THE WORK!**

32 He that spared not his own Son, but delivered him up for us all, how shall he not with him also freely give us all things?

33 Who shall lay anything to the charge of God's elect? *It is* God that justifieth.

34 Who *is* he that condemneth? *It is* Christ that died, yea rather, that is risen again, who is even at the right hand of God, who also maketh intercession for us.

35 **Who (WHAT ENEMY)**shall separate us from the love of Christ? *shall* tribulation, or distress, or persecution, or famine, or nakedness, or peril, or sword?

36 As it is written, For thy sake we are killed all the day long; we are accounted as sheep for the slaughter.

37 Nay, in all these things we are more than conquerors **through him (THE ENEMY HAS TO COME THROUGH OUR JESUS FIRST)** that loved us.

38 For I am **persuaded**, (CONFIDENT) that neither death, nor life, nor angels, nor principalities, nor powers, nor things present, nor things to come,

39 Nor height, nor depth, nor any other creature, **shall be able to separate us from the love of God,** (THERE IS NO FEAR IN LOVE) which is in Christ Jesus our Lord. CAN'T BE SEPARATED FROM HIS LOVE, **BUT SIN SEPARATES US FROM HIS PRESENCE .** OUR

PROMISE AND PROMOTION IS ON THE OTHER SIDE OF OUR AFFLICTION, STAND!

"The Glory Of Death"

THE EVIDENCE OF A PROSPEROUS SOUL

3 JOHN 1:2

Beloved, I wish above all things that thou mayest prosper
and be in health, even as thy soul prospereth.

GOD'S PLAN IS FOR ALL TO BE RICH, WHICH SIMPLY MEANS TO HAVE MORE THAN ENOUGH, BEGINS WITH A PROSPEROUS SOUL. WE MUST DESTROY THE IMAGE THAT LACK OF WEALTH HAS PRODUCED.

PROV 4:23 Keep thy heart with all diligence; for out of it *are* the issues of life.

I must guard my heart, for it determines the course, boundaries of my life.

PS. 1:1-2 Blessed *is* the man that walketh not in the counsel of the ungodly, nor standeth in the way of sinners, nor sitteth in the seat of the scornful.

2 But his delight *is* in the law of the LORD; and in his law doth he meditate day and night. Meditation is God's process by which I renew my mind. (MEDITATION OF GOD'S WORD RIDS THE INFECTION/ WORRY) The tree is what is being produced (FRUIT). I must SEE prosperity, to BECOME prosperous. IT **BEGINS TO BE** , IN ME!

***DECLARE WHAT GOD SAYS AT ALL TIMES! WHAT GOD SAID, GOD SAW. REVELATION - WHAT I SEE, I MUST SAY!

*** I WILL NEVER PROSPER IN THE NATURAL, BEYOND THE PROSPERITY OF MY SOUL. (MIND, WILL, IMAGINATION, EMOTIONS, INTELECT) PHIL 2:3 For it is God (THE WORD) which worketh in you both to will (DESIRE) and to do (BECOME) of *his* good pleasure.

PS. 35:37 Let them shout for joy, and be glad, that favour my righteous cause: yea, let them say continually, Let the LORD be magnified, which hath pleasure in the prosperity of his servant.

JOHN 10:10 The thief cometh not, but for to steal, and to kill, and to destroy: I am come that they might have life, and that they might have *it* more abundantly.

PS. 115:14 The LORD shall increase you more and more, you and your children.

1 CORN . 4:8 Now ye are full, now ye are rich, ye have reigned as kings without us: and I would to God ye did reign, that we also might reign with you.

MATT. 13 19 When any one heareth the word of the kingdom, and understandeth *it* not, (NO INSIGHT, NO REVELATION) then cometh the wicked *one*, and catcheth away that which was sown in his heart. This is he which received seed by the wayside. MEDITATING REVELATION RENEWS/PROSPERS /INCREASES MY SOUL! PETER HAD RECEIVED A REVELATION,

THE WORD OF GOD CHANGES THE WAY WE SEE IT. ***KINGDOM MINDED!

ROM. 14:17 For the kingdom of God is not meat and drink; but righteousness, peace, and joy in the Holy Ghost.

PS. 103:19-21 The LORD hath prepared his throne in the heavens; and HIS kingdom ruleth over all.

20 Bless the LORD, ye his angels, that excel in strength, that do his commandments, hearkening unto the voice of his word.

21 Bless ye the LORD, all *ye* his hosts; *ye* ministers of his, that do his pleasure.

MATT. 26:52-53 Then said Jesus unto him, Put up again thy sword into his place: for all they that take the sword shall perish with the sword.

53 Thinkest thou that I cannot now pray to my Father, and he shall presently give me more than twelve legions of angels?

2 KINGS 6:15-17 And when the servant of the man of God was risen early, and gone forth, behold, an host compassed the city both with horses and chariots. And his servant said unto him, Alas, my master! how shall we do?

16 And he answered, Fear not: for they that *be* with us *are* more than they that *be* with them. I MUST SEE THE KINGDOM

17 And Elisha prayed, and said, LORD, I pray thee, open his eyes, that he may see. And the LORD opened the eyes of the young man; and he saw: and, behold, the mountain *was* full of horses and chariots of fire round about Elisha. SHADOW OF THE KINGDOM.

EX. 23:20-23 Behold, I send an Angel before thee, to keep thee in the way, and to bring thee into the place which I have prepared.

21 Beware of him, and obey his voice, provoke him not; for he will not pardon your transgressions: for my name *is* in him.

22 But if thou shalt indeed obey his voice, and do all that I speak then I will be an enemy unto thine enemies, and an adversary unto thine adversaries.

23 For mine Angel shall go before thee, and bring thee in unto the Amorites, and the Hittites, and the Perizzites, and the Canaanites, the Hivites, and the Jebusites: and I will cut them off. RECEIVE AND SEE!

NUMBERS 13: 30-33 And Caleb stilled the people before Moses, and said, Let us go up at once, and possess it; for we are well able to overcome it.

31 But the men that went up with him said, We be not able to go up against the people; for they *are* stronger than we.

32 And they brought up an evil report of the land which they had searched unto the children of Israel, saying, The land, through which we have gone to search it, *is* a land that eateth up the inhabitants thereof; and all the people that we saw in it *are* men of a great stature. LEADERS BROUGHT BACK AN EVIL.NEGATIVE REPORT

**14:1 And all the congregation lifted up their voice, and cried; and the people wept that night. BECAUSE OF WHAT THE LEADERS TAUGHT.

33 And there we saw the giants, the sons of Anak, *which come* of the giants: and we were in our own sight as grasshoppers, and so we were in their sight.

MATT. 15:14 Let them alone: they be blind leaders of the blind. And if the blind lead the blind, both shall fall into the ditch. BLIND LEADERS OF THE BLIND. NO REVELATION. CAN ONLY TAKE PEOPLE AS FAR AS THEY CAN SEE.

**TO TRANSFORM THE WORLD, WE MUST FIRST BE TRANSFORMED!

MATT. 18:19-20 Again I say unto you, That if two of you shall agree on earth as touching any thing that they shall ask, it shall be done for them of my Father which is in heaven.

20 For where two or three are gathered together in my name, there am I in the midst of them. TWO AGREE GOD MAKES IT A LAW AND DRAWS A LINE THAT THE ENEMY CAN'T CROSS!

JERM. 23:1 Woe be unto the pastors that destroy and scatter the sheep of my pasture! saith the LORD. WE MUST TEACH/PREACH THE KINGDOM

MATT. 23:13 But woe unto you, scribes and Pharisees, hypocrites! for ye shut up the kingdom of heaven against men: for ye neither go in *yourselves,* neither suffer ye them that are entering to go in. THEY DIDN'T GO AND BLOCK OTHERS FROM THE KINGDOM, THIS DISPLEASES GOD!

MATT. 24:14 And this gospel of the kingdom shall be preached in all the world for a witness unto all nations; and then shall the end come. THE KINGDOM HAS ITS OWN ABILITY TO DO WHAT IT SAYS. POWER AND AUTHORITY!

2 CORN. 5:17 Therefore if any man *be* in Christ, *he is* a new creature: old things are passed away; behold, all things are become new.

JOHN 1:10-14 He was in the world, and the world was made by him, and the world knew him not.

11 He came unto his own, and his own received him not.

12 But as many as received him, to them gave he **POWER TO BECOME** the **SONS of GOD**, *even* to them that believe on his name:

13 Which were born, not of blood, nor of the will of the flesh, nor of the will of man, **but of God. BORN OF THE WORD**

14 And the **Word was made flesh**, and dwelt among us, (and we beheld his glory, the glory as of the only begotten of the Father,) full of grace and truth. **TRANSFORMED!!!!**

THE POINT OF NO RETURN!

FROM A CATERPILLAR

TO

A BUTTERFLY

TO GOD BE THE GLORY!

www.ingramcontent.com/pod-product-compliance
Lightning Source LLC
Chambersburg PA
CBHW071158130626
46553CB00004B/1712